DEATH VALLEY

By the same author

DEATH VALLEY

BY GEORGE LAYCOCK

FOUR WINDS PRESS   NEW YORK

Library of Congress Cataloging in Publication Data

Laycock, George.
  Death Valley.

  Bibliography: p.
  Includes index.
  SUMMARY: Traces the history of Death Valley and discusses the
minerals, plants, and animals to be found there.
  1. Death Valley—Juvenile literature.   2. Natural
history—California—Death Valley.   [1. Death Valley.
2. Natural history—California—Death Valley]   I. Title.
F868.D2L32   979.4′87   75–42276
ISBN 0–590–07399–0

Published by Four Winds Press
A Division of Scholastic Magazines, Inc., New York, N.Y.
Copyright © 1976 by George Laycock

1   2   3   4   5   80   79   78   77   76

CONTENTS

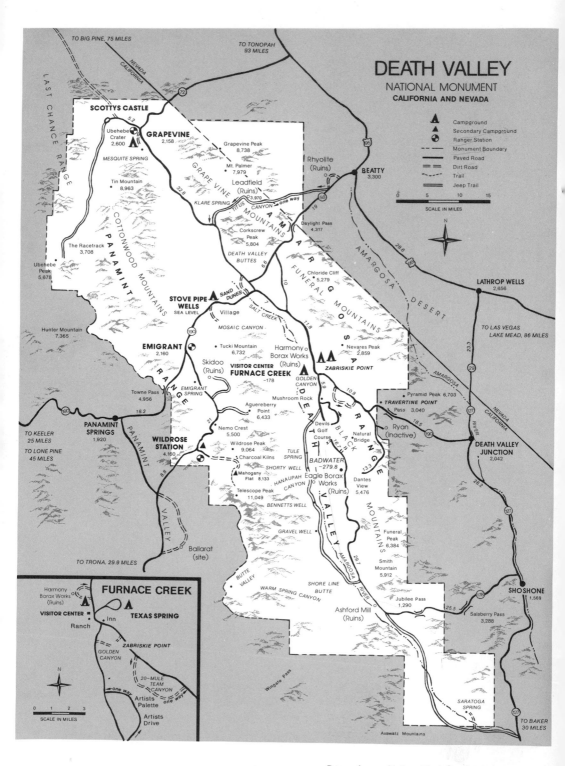

Drawn from a National Park Service map

INTRODUCTION

 *More than half a million visitors come each year to the heart of Death Valley. They come to see this wilderness of sand and rock* where early explorers faced death from thirst and the furnacelike heat. They discover a land rich in spectacular scenery. And if they look closely, they find a remarkable number of native plants and animals that survive in this harsh world.

With each new visit to Death Valley we make new discoveries. The National Monument covers nearly three thousand square miles, a desert unlike that found anywhere else. We have stood on the high places to look down upon the flat fields of the valley floor lying white with salt. We have traveled the hidden canyons, photographed the flowers of spring, and explored historic sites.

Many scientists and historians have studied the mysteries of Death Valley. This story of the famous valley is drawn from their discoveries too. Perhaps it will refresh memories for those who have been there, and, for others, serve as an introduction to one of the world's truly remarkable desert regions.

1. DREAMS OF DISTANT LANDS

 As he went about his work in his father's store, John Colton listened to the conversations of the customers. He heard them tell about the health of their cattle and the condition of their corn fields in the flat and fertile lands around Galesburg, Illinois. There was talk of weather and the right time for planting wheat and how to cure hogs of cholera.

These were subjects John had heard all his life. But in that year of 1848 men came in to the store talking about another subject, one that excited John far more than farming. They spoke of gold. This magic word rolled off young John Colton's tongue with a beautiful ring. It was as if he could see the heavy yellow nuggets glistening in the sun. A man could become rich picking them up!

In addition, gold promised new exciting adventures. Gold had been discovered near the western edge of the land in the distant hills of California. Now that would be a trip! John could picture the scene every time another family rolled through town headed west in their creaking wagons. He could see broad rolling landscapes of prairie grass rippled by the soft summer winds. Towering mountains pushed their snow white peaks into the blue sky.

There would be nights beneath the western stars, nights of songs and stories around flickering yellow campfires. And there would be a new adventure for each day. Sometimes, thinking about it, John Colton could scarcely keep his mind on his work, and more than likely his father spoke to him often about mistakes in figuring the prices for beans, crackers, and nails that his customers came in to purchase.

The more he heard of gold, the more convinced the seventeen-year-old grocery clerk became that he was going west, and soon. He began turning his thoughts to practical matters. What equipment would he need? When was the best time to start? Other young men were also catching the gold fever and John soon found neighbors who were eager to join him.

When all was ready, there were between thirty and forty men in the group, most of them young. They drove twelve heavily loaded wagons drawn by oxen. They had saddle horses, tools, spare parts, food, guns, and ammunition. They even had extra oxen to replace those that gave out along the trail.

The day of their departure approached and the spirits of the gold seekers soared. They named their group the "Jayhawkers" and swore oaths of allegiance, promising to share all their goods and stick together no matter how difficult the journey might become. On April 5, 1849, as John Colton and his Jayhawkers spoke to their oxen and filed out of Galesburg, other wagons were traveling with them. Still others would join them along the way, and from time to time, some would leave and strike out on their own routes. But the Jayhawkers stayed together—until they came to the most difficult part of the trip, a hidden valley as hot and dry as a furnace.

Travel with oxen and wagons was painfully slow. Fifteen miles a day was considered good speed as the creaking wheels rolled over the rutted trails. For food the travelers had wild deer, wild turkeys, and wild prairie chickens, which were abundant on the grasslands. At Council Bluffs, Iowa, they faced the broad waters of the Missouri River. They had to raft their equipment over to the western shore a little at a time. Nearly a week was spent in the crossing.

Day after day the distance to the promised goldfields gradually shrank beneath the iron-rimmed wheels of the Jayhawker wagons. These young travelers from Illinois were enjoying their trip, but they thought often of others already in California staking the best claims, and they urged their oxen onward.

With a larger party they finally departed from Salt Lake City, Utah. There was singing around campfires, and strangers became friends. The country through which they passed was new and exciting. And always there was the lure of gold.

But there was also an impatience running through the group. Weeks had passed since their journey began and still, in Utah, they were hundreds of miles from the goldfields of California. Around the campfires and at rest stops they spoke often of the trail they were following. Their route lay by way of the Spanish Trail, which turned south to go around the high mountains. This meant that once California was reached, the gold seekers would have to travel north again up the west side of the mountains. Perhaps, if a person could only find the route, there was a way directly west, through the mountains. Such a route would cut hundreds of miles and weeks of travel from the journey. But the people dreaming of such a shortcut knew nothing of the country.

Neither did they know much about survival in the wilderness.

Their captain was Jefferson Hunt, a hardened traveler who knew the Spanish Trail. He also understood the risk in leaving the trail to search for a shorter way through the mountains. He knew that some families were thinking of leaving the group to head off directly west. It was, he believed, a foolish mistake, but there was little he could do if they insisted on risking their lives on an unknown trail.

Maps were scarce. The one the travelers were following was supplied by the United States Government and was known as the Fremont map because it had been drawn by Lt. John Charles Fremont. Fremont, nicknamed "the Pathfinder," had explored in the West between the Rocky Mountains and the Pacific

Surrounded by desert mountains, seemingly stacked one upon the other, early Death Valley travelers fought heat and thirst and recognized little of beauty.

Ocean. It was while he was in the Army Topographical Corps that Fremont prepared the map which the west-bound travelers carried and to which they often referred. There was one serious omission on the Fremont map, however. It did not show the broad and barren deserts that lie on both sides of the Panamint Mountains.

Another map figured heavily in their decision to turn due west away from the Spanish Trail. This map was a crude drawing that one of the men claimed he had bought from an Indian chief. The chief had picked up a stick and sketched the route in the sand, and the man had then copied it onto paper. Historians think that the Ute chief was using the map only to brag about how he had escaped when he went on horse-stealing raids in California.

Would he have shared his real escape route? No one knew. But the gold seekers wanted to believe, and so they did.

While still in Utah the Spanish Trail cut sharply south at a point known as Mountain Meadows. It was here that the whole group assembled around a big campfire on the night of November 3, 1848, to talk about whether or not they should take the shortcut.

Half a century later John W. Brier recalled, in newspaper interviews, details of how the party split and went their separate ways. The new map showing the shortcut held strong appeal. If it could be trusted, as more and more people wanted to believe, they should follow its dotted lines. Along the way springs were marked, and the trip was said to require only two weeks' time, far less than would be needed to follow Captain Hunt along the twisting, roundabout Spanish Trail looping far to the south.

John Brier, who was a child at the time, was afraid of the silent, grim-looking guide. "I wondered if he ever loved anybody," Brier recalled, "and if he slept on horseback." Hunt had seldom spoken to the men of the wagon train as day after day he grimly led them along the trail. They had agreed to pay him $1,000 for leading them to Los Angeles in nine weeks.

As the others assembled around the big campfire and talked excitedly of the new trail, Captain Hunt had little to say. His route lay along the Spanish Trail and as long as a single wagon wanted to go the southern route he intended to lead it. At the campfire meeting he did make one brief speech after listening to the people discuss the advantages of going directly toward the mountains. "All I have to say," he told them sourly, "is that if you take that route you will all be landed in Hell."

The long train had started out with one hundred and five wagons. "As a result of the conference," wrote Brier, "Captain Hunt was left with a following of five wagons, while we pushed on without a guide, without a chart. As early as the second day our trail began to swerve too far south." Among those hurrying on directly toward the forbidding mountains were the Jayhawkers. Already the more timid among the travelers began to harbor nagging doubts that the shortcut was, after all, a good idea.

2. THE PATHFINDERS

 *The trail became more difficult for the wagons and more than once the whole party stopped while scouts were sent out to seek* better routes. They stayed beside one canyon for two days trying to find a route across. Many, already discouraged, turned back at this point and hurried to catch up again with Captain Hunt. But there were still twenty-seven wagons headed west, searching for a new trail. The Jayhawkers were among them. These young men, however, wanted to travel fast. They wanted no families with women and children tagging along to slow them down, and they said so. The family of Rev. J. W. Brier, however, went with them even if they were not welcome.

Mrs. Brier, the first white woman ever to enter Death Valley, became a heroine to the group. She was a small woman, weighing perhaps one hundred and fifteen pounds as the journey began. William Lewis Manly wrote of her strength and courage in his *Death Valley In '49*. "She was the one who put the packs on the oxen in the morning. She it was who took them off at night, built the fires, cooked the food, helped the children, and did all sorts of work when the father of the family was too tired, which was most of the time. . . . It was entirely due to her undying devotion that her husband and children lived."

Other families started off on their own with their wagons and oxen. Among them were Asa Bennett and J. B. Arcane and their families. Also traveling with Bennett were two remarkable young men. One was John Rogers, a large, strong mountaineer from Tennessee. The other was a tall, thin man named William Lewis Manly, who had met Asa Bennett in Salt Lake City. Manly and Rogers wanted to join a westbound party headed for the gold-fields, and Bennett welcomed them into his little family group where they could help with the driving and whatever other work there was to do.

Where Furnace Creek Inn stands today, like a yellow adobe fortress in the desert, there also stands a stone monument beside the road. It marks the place where the Forty-Niners came down into Death Valley. Standing on this site the weary travelers stared out upon the valley with sinking hopes. Before them was spread the hot dry basin with its salt flats and bare earth baking beneath the desert sun. Across the valley the mountains stood bold and high, like an unbroken wall erected to block their prog-ress. They studied the peaks and snowy ridges, seeking a pass where ox-drawn wagons might cross to the other side. But the mountains seemed solid and unbroken.

In this trackless desert below sea level the travelers began suffering greater hardships than they ever imagined possible. The Jayhawkers had sent out their scouts only to have them return reporting that they could find no way through the mountains. The trail in the heart of the valley was soon littered with equip-ment cast out to lighten the burden on the starving and thirsty oxen. Finally, the Jayhawkers, followed by the Briers, hurried on and out of sight.

In the early morning the members of the Bennett and Arcane

families hitched their oxen and began moving their seven creaking wagons through the last of the canyons leading down into the flat valley floor. They turned their oxen toward the south end of the valley where the mountains seemed to be lower against the desert sky.

The little party crossed the rough salt flats with jolting wagons moving slowly along behind weary, over-worked oxen. By the time they reached the west side of the valley they were thirsty, hungry, weary, and discouraged. There were deep fears among them that their lives would end in this unfriendly desert. Besides, they knew they were lost and that no one would come to their rescue.

They stumbled on mile after mile, until at last they could go no farther. "We had a few small pieces of dry bread," wrote one of them later. "This we kept for the children giving them a little now and then." By this time they were killing and eating their oxen to stay alive. They had guns and ammunition but, as one said, "We had seen no living creature in this desert." Then, they came to one of the rare springs of fresh water in Death Valley.

Later they held another meeting and out of it came a final, desperate scheme. Mr. Bennett outlined his idea. "I propose," he explained, "that we select two of our youngest, strongest men and ask them to go ahead on foot to try to seek a settlement and food, and we will go back to the good spring we have just left and wait for their return."

William Lewis Manly had done much of the pathfinding work for the party and had proved himself trustworthy and reliable. The group chose Manly and the rugged, big man from the Tennessee country, John Rogers, to try to cross the mountains for

Flanking a dry stream bed in the heart of Death Valley are the gullied slopes of sunbaked mountains.

help. Together these two left and, shouldering packs that held their supply of ox meat, one blanket between them, and a gun for each, set off toward the distant snow-capped peaks to the west. Some thought they could get beyond the mountains and perhaps bring help within ten days.

The next day Manly and Rogers were out of water, and they found no spring, lake, or seep where they might refill their canteens. They walked for miles, sometimes making sidetrips where a spot of green grass on a mountainside seemed to promise water. But time after time there was no water except what they could chew from the moist stems of a few blades of grass. The only promising stream they encountered gurgled down the slope toward a beautiful little lake. They fell on their knees but found in the first big drink that it was very salty.

Once more they made a camp and spent a miserable night. The following day Manly and Rogers walked in silence because talking dried their mouths out even more. They became so thirsty they could not swallow the meat they carried. "It seemed," wrote Manly, "we were going to die with plenty of food in our hands, because we could not eat it." Neither would their thirst let them sleep. They thought of nothing any longer but water. "No one who has never felt the extreme of thirst," Manly wrote, "can imagine the distress, the despair, which it brings."

The new morning brought the old picture back. This was desolate, dry country where death by thirst stalked all travelers. Manly and Rogers, afraid they might miss a source of water, split up and explored separate canyons along their way, promising to fire a shot if one of them should find water. It was not yet full light and the canyons were bitterly cold at this elevation. Soon Manly heard

Rogers' gun and when he reached him, he found where a thin sheet of ice had formed on the sand. Another hour beneath the climbing sun and this water too would have vanished in the sand.

This ice probably saved their lives. Once they had eaten the ice they brought out the food they had been unable to swallow. They soon felt strong once again, and they looked hopefully at the towering mountain peak still miles away.

Manly and Rogers, throughout their journey, had been alert for signs of fires or tracks that might reveal the presence of the Indians. The Shoshones in the area had shown nothing but signs of hostility toward the invaders of 1849. Three oxen had been shot with arrows. A few times Indians had been spotted slipping away from the edge of their camps. Manly still remembered the day his party found a store of squash left by the Indians and thoughtlessly stole all the food and ate it. He wished that instead they had left the food for its rightful owners. In this harsh land any stealing of food would certainly be viewed as reason for revenge.

One night they sighted another camp ahead of them. There was no way of knowing at first whether it was an Indian camp. They crept toward the fire as silently as coyotes. Manly noted that there was no sound of barking Indian dogs. This was a good sign. Finally, within easy gunshot, they cocked their firearms and decided to call out to the people in the camp. A midwestern voice answered. In the camp were members of the Jayhawkers. They too were walking out of Death Valley and on this night they were fortunate to camp beside a little spring of fresh water. Their canteen had been empty for four days. No longer did this group of young men joke among themselves. "The whole camp,"

Manly recalled, "was silent, and all seemed to realize their situation. Before them was a level plain . . . so broad as to take five or six days to cross." There seemed little promise of finding much water in that desert.

But Manly and Rogers left early the next morning, not headed south with the others, but still west toward the snow-covered mountains. There was not time for them to take the southern route if they were to save their party. "For the first time," Manly said later, "it really seemed there was very little hope for us." The others felt the same about the southern course and a number of them gave Manly the names of their families and asked him to notify them if the opportunity ever came.

Rogers and Manly crossed the mountain range. They came upon good signs, and saw a distant grove of cottonwoods, then larger trees, and finally a beautiful, gurgling brook of cold, pure water.

But they were still far from help. They discussed returning for their party and bringing them out this far, but decided instead to try to take a supply of food back to them. Their route led through a tangled thicket for many miles. But a few more days' travel brought them to a splendid scene where hundreds of cattle grazed over a fertile valley floor. They had reached the edge of civilization. "Tears of joy ran down our faces," Manly wrote many years later in his book.

They were soon discovered by a group of ranch workers. By this time they were about thirty miles from Los Angeles and five hundred miles from San Francisco. They acquired three horses and a mule and were given food to take back into the desert.

They moved with their new animals back into the hills. The

Evaporating waters of an ancient lake left behind this broad, flat region of rock-hard, crystallized salt known as the Devil's Golf Course.

high desert was as harsh and unfriendly and the water as scarce as before. As the miles wore on, the hardy mule held up well, but the horses grew weaker and weaker. Manly and Rogers were deeply worried now about the people they had left in the desert. The ten days had long since passed and perhaps the little group had made one last futile effort to escape the valley only to perish of thirst or be killed by Indians along the way. To speed their return the two men again changed their route, heading directly up a rugged, rocky canyon, hoping to cut several days from their travels and reach the waiting families now only fifty miles to the east.

Their route wound through a tumbled land of huge boulders and along narrow cliffside trails. The trail grew increasingly narrow and difficult. Finally, Manly and Rogers had no choice but to leave their horses, which were now too weak to carry anything but their saddles. Still the little mule plodded on, carefully picking a route along treacherous narrow cliffs where a single false step would dash her to death on the rocks below. Besides, she knew enough about desert living to pass up no blade of grass found near the trail.

Eventually Manly and Rogers and their mule crossed over the last mountain. They could look down again upon the dreaded valley. "About noon," Manly wrote, "we came in sight of the wagons, still a long way off, but in the clear air we could make them out and tell what they were. . . ." Not until they were within half a mile could they see the wagons close-up, because the camp was in a little depression. Fear gripped the young explorers. The camp looked deserted. Perhaps, thought Manly, the Indians had exacted their revenge for the theft of the squashes. Perhaps, too, the Indians lay in ambush waiting for them.

They were within a hundred yards of the wagons and still no sign of life greeted them. Manly lifted his rifle and fired a shot into the air. For some moments nothing changed. No life showed. "Then as if by magic a man came out from under a wagon and stood up, looking all around . . . then he threw his arms up high over his head and shouted, 'The boys have come! The boys have come!'" Manly and Rogers had been twenty-six days on the trail.

When the weeping ceased and the first excitement of the reunion was over, they hurriedly made plans for their trip out of the valley. For the first time in days these stranded men, women, and children began to believe again that they would not die here, far from their homes, on these treacherous sands. One can imagine the thoughts that must have filled their minds.

Some of them had given up on Manly and Rogers. One who had become impatient was Henry Wade. He had hitched his oxen one day, loaded his family into the creaking wagon, and left the camp. Instead of heading west toward the snow-capped peaks, Wade turned his oxen southward. This was a fortunate decision. Near the south end of the valley the Wades saw a green marsh and found there beautiful springs holding all the fresh water they could use. They also encountered wild game. Rested and refreshed, they left the springs. Today we know these waters as Saratoga Springs. Once out of Death Valley they began to live better. Still traveling south, the party came to the Mojave River and began following it. In this way they had water when they needed it. Water also attracts wildlife, and this gave the Wade family game on which to dine.

Eventually they came to ranching country and friendly people and still, unlike the traveling companions they had left back in the hated desert valley, they had their wagon and the family possessions it carried. The Wades were the only ones among that group of Forty-Niners to escape Death Valley without loss of their family goods.

The Bennetts and Arcanes soon learned from Manly and Rogers that, to follow the route they had scouted, they must still travel two hundred and fifty miles through extremely rugged territory, and that there was no hope of taking their wagons. Up out of the valley, the women and children rode on the backs of the remaining oxen while the little mule carried much of the food and other supplies still left. Behind them they left every pound of weight they could do without.

From almost every part of the valley, these weary travelers viewed a splendid, towering mountain, the highest peak in the range. Visitors today know it as Telescope Peak, 11,049 feet above sea level.

The little group struggled over the rocky slopes to the top of the Panamint Mountains. There, at last, surrounded by the clean, cool snow and refreshed by the mountain breeze, the weary families stopped to rest. Turning back in the direction they had come, they looked down again into the fiery trough between the mountain ranges. Quietly Mrs. Bennett said, "Goodbye, Death Valley," and Death Valley it has been ever since.

The Bennetts and Arcanes, led by the two men who had saved their lives, came out of Death Valley and eventually down out of the mountains. Once more they found food and water and a new hope for life. But as long as they lived, not one would ever forget the grim days and nights suffered in the heart of the unknown valley into which they had stumbled.

Finally, John Colton, the other Jayhawkers, and the Briers came out of Death Valley, too. They had lost all the oxen and equipment with which they began their journey in the Midwest.

Fifty-three years later Colton was quoted in the *San Francisco Bulletin* as he spoke of those frightening weeks in the famous valley. "For three months," he said, "we were lost in the desert, most of the time hunting for water. . . . Finally, on the fourth of February the remnant of our party . . . mere walking skeletons, ravenous and some nearly crazy, struck God's country on the Old Fort Tejon Trail." Spanish cowboys discovered them there and fed them until they regained their strength.

When Mrs. Brier was eighty-nine she was living in Lodi, California. Three of the original Jayhawkers, including John Colton, went there to hold a reunion. They discussed again the terrible days in Death Valley, times still fresh in their minds after half a century.

Remarkably, only one of the people wandering about in the valley during that winter of 1849 died in the heart of the valley. Some died upon the trail leaving the valley, however, and none of the others ever forgot the hunger, thirst, weariness, and fear of their pioneering venture into this place which the Indians called "Ground Afire."

The valley called "death" is today very much alive. Thousands of visitors come every year to camp, hike across the sand, and loaf in the sunshine of this strange and scenic valley, which has become one of the world's most famous desert lands.

3. THE NATURE OF DEATH VALLEY

 *Its visitors today come from distant places. They may come from country shaded by towering forest trees or covered with an endless expanse of prairie grass.* Or they live by the seashore with its endless waves and sea breezes.

Death Valley is a foreign world to such visitors as they stand in the salt flats on the valley floor or gaze down from high overlooks in the barren hills. Through a haze of dust they view perhaps the hottest and driest scene on earth. The contrast between such a remarkable desert world and their distant homes is stark and real.

For one hundred and ninety miles this arid land stretches north and south between its mountain walls. The valley is from five to twenty miles wide. Within it lie five hundred and fifty-five square miles of land lower than the surface of the oceans. At one point, near Badwater, Death Valley's floor is two hundred and eighty-two feet below sea level, lower than anywhere else throughout the Western Hemisphere.

This is dry country, the driest in North America. One definition of a desert is land that averages less than ten inches of precipitation a year. Death Valley averages less than two inches. For sixty years, from 1910 to 1970, the average annual rainfall was 1.66 inches. In one year, 1929, official records show that no rain at all fell in Death Valley. There may be occasional showers that hardly dampen the sand. One afternoon such a shower came over a small section of the valley where we were driving. Drops of water mixed with the dust on the windshield but there was not enough to wash the glass. Sometimes rain falling through the hot desert air evaporates and never reaches the ground.

Deserts may receive their entire year's rainfall in one or two spectacular storms. Torrents of water fall upon the parched earth. Dry streambeds, called arroyos, suddenly fill with tumbling muddy water and overflow in flash floods. Animals that have survived months of drought in their burrows are suddenly drowned. Then there may be no more rain for weeks or months.

Visitors to the desert sometimes find themselves asking what it is that makes the world so different there. What really causes deserts? Why do they receive so little rain, other lands so much?

Across the southwestern United States and reaching south into Mexico there are four remarkable deserts that together form the North American Desert. Largest of these is the Great Basin Desert lying between the Rocky Mountains and the Sierra Nevadas from central Oregon to Wyoming, then south deep into Utah and Nevada. Much of the Great Basin is grassland and sagebrush lying at elevations above three thousand feet. Far to the south is the Chihuahuan Desert of Mexico, Texas, and New Mexico, a dry, hot land rich in cacti. In addition, there is the Sonoran Desert of southern California, Arizona, and Mexico where the saguaro, the biggest cactus, may stand fifty feet high, weigh ten tons, and live for two hundred and fifty years. The Mohave Des-

Earthquakes helped form the moonlike landscape of Death Valley.

ert lies mostly in California and Nevada, and Death Valley is in the heart of it.

Deserts have developed in geographic locations that are cut off from sources of rainfall. Moisture rides inland from the oceans on the prevailing winds. Some deserts lie secluded on the leeward side (the side situated away from the wind) of high mountain ranges, which stand like a giant curtain between these dry lands and the oceans. Death Valley and the desert lands around it are cut off from the Pacific Ocean's moisture by the towering peaks of the Sierra Nevada Mountains. As the ocean winds flow in against the mountains, much of the moisture they carry condenses and falls. This may make the slopes facing the ocean, the coastal mountain ranges, so heavily watered they become rain forests.

But the winds, no longer carrying water, sweep up and over the mountains. They cross to the other side, bringing little if any moisture to the inland regions, which are said to lie in rain shadows.

Some great deserts, however, are found where there are no mountains to "short-stop" the rain. Cold ocean currents sweeping along the edge of a continent may help create such deserts as the Atacama, one of the world's driest deserts. It is the result of the Humboldt current flowing along the coast of Chile in South America. These cold currents cool the winds moving inland, condense their moisture, and leave only dry winds to cross the thirsty land.

One scorching day in 1922, at Azizia in the Sahara Desert of northern Africa, the official thermometer recorded a temperature of 136.4 degrees F. This stands as the world record. But in Death

Valley, there is a record of a day almost as hot, 134 degrees. These temperatures are taken five feet above ground level in the shade!

The closer you get to the ground on a hot day, the higher the temperature becomes. At ground level, where the snakes and lizards live, scientists have recorded temperatures as high as 201 degrees. Understandably, most of the desert's animal life must seek protection from such heat.

Fortunately, the top layer of desert sand, like the air, is dry. Its water has been replaced by air. And air is a good insulator, while water is an excellent conductor of heat. So the day's heat does not penetrate deeply into the earth and there is refuge underground for many of the desert's creatures.

Just as the desert warms rapidly during the day, it is quick to cool at night. Night temperatures may be 30 degrees lower than those of the afternoon before. At one location in the Sahara Desert the temperature once fell 100 degrees within the same day, from 126 degrees to 26.

The upper levels of the dry desert air are sharp and clear, and day after day the skies are blue. Because of this, more of the sun's heat reaches the earth than in other regions where there are clouds, dust, and smog between the sun and earth. Similarly, at night there are few clouds above the deserts and little dust in the air to hold back the heat escaping from the earth.

Elsewhere, beyond the deserts, the canopy of woodlands or the carpet of grass helps break the force of the sun's rays and provides a cool shaded environment. But in the desert, because of the wide spacing of the plants, much of the land is directly exposed to the sun's rays.

The face of Death Valley is a record of the earth's natural his-

Death Valley is a harsh desert shaped by the elements over hundreds of years.

tory. For the geologist, a thousand years is almost insignificant. A million years is not yet yesterday. Scientists can measure rates of decay of elements that decay slowly and establish approximate ages. Such studies of the rocks show the earth to be about four and a half *billion* years old.

Earth's history is divided by scientists into great segments of time. First came the Precambrian Era, that era between the birth of the earth and the first appearance of complex life forms. About eighty percent of the earth's past is hidden in that era. Next was the Paleozoic Era, then the Mesozoic, followed by the age of recent life, the Cenozoic Era. Rocks from all of these times are found in the formations of Death Valley, making this arid and hot region an outdoor laboratory for those who study the forces that shaped the earth.

As the centuries passed, massive forces changed this region. Ancient seas came and went. Mountains rose and tilted in various directions. Layers of rocks bent and folded and were forced together in giant layers. Over the years the pressure of massive weights helped to change the nature of some of these rocks until their stories are mixed and sometimes confusing.

On the west side of the valley are the towering Panamint Mountains. Telescope Peak, standing 11,049 feet above sea level, is the highest peak in the Death Valley area. But in the Paleozoic Era the Panamints were at the bottom of an ancient sea. Across the valley to the east stand the somewhat lower ridges of the Black Mountains, part of the Amargosa Range. On both sides of the valley these mountains have faulted and tilted toward the east.

Death Valley is not a typical valley cut by a stream. Instead it was formed by faulting. As the earth shifted and sank, rock layers beneath the valley floor settled deeper and deeper while the mountains continued to rise. These may have been slow movements, underway for long periods of time.

At several times through the ages seas flooded the valley. The broad sea of the Precambrian Era deposited layers of sediment that became sedimentary rocks. Then came a time of erosion to be followed by the return of the sea. This lasted through the Paleozoic Era, and new layers of sediment, thousands of feet thick, were deposited on the sea floor. Within the rocks that formed from the oldest of these sediments, men would one day find lead, zinc, and silver. In addition, these rocks were capped by dolomite and limestone believed to have formed in the sea-water through chemical precipitation.

This ancient valley has also felt the force of volcanoes, and visitors to Death Valley can still see the evidence. The map on display at the National Monument headquarters shows the Ubehebe Crater in the Monument's northern section. This crater is half a mile across and about six hundred and sixty feet deep, and hikers may follow trails down into it. Ubehebe and smaller craters in the vicinity are reminders of the most recent Death Valley volcanic activity, perhaps within the last thousand years. These craters were created by violence. The magma, or molten lava, rising toward the surface through fissures in the earth's rock layers, finally reached the underground water level. The heat of the magma turned the water to steam, and the explosive force of steam created the craters. If you drive along Artists Drive, which is a loop road on the east side of the valley, you can see other volcanic rocks.

As we drove south from Furnace Creek toward Badwater, a low cliff appeared along the base of the Black Mountains on our left. This ten-foot cliff was here before the road was built and before modern man first arrived in the valley. Scientists, puzzled about this cliff, finally decided that it was formed by faulting as the earth shifted and fractured.

About two thousand years ago, the geologists say, there was a broad, flat lake lying in the valley floor. This lake had once been larger and deeper but the climate was already becoming drier and hotter and the lake was slowly vanishing.

Look to the mountain canyons opening onto the valley on either side. From the mouth of these canyons there are broad, sloping fields of earth and rocks that washed out of the gorges. These alluvial fans were the result of cloudbursts in the mountains. Waters rushed into the narrow gorges and surged through the rocky canyons, carrying heavy loads of earth and rock from the canyon. As the waters spread over a broader area, they lost their force and the heavier materials stopped to form the fan-shaped slopes at the foot of the mountain canyons. The largest alluvial fans are found on the western side of the valley. They display a variety of colors. The lighter colored ones are said to be the youngest, because the older alluvial fans have had sufficient time to turn dark and acquire a black polish known as desert varnish.

4. THE GOLD SEEKERS

Today's prospectors, and there are dozens of them poking around the lonely canyons of Death Valley, no longer resemble the old- time desert rat with his plodding burro. The tough little burro has been replaced by a four-wheel drive, off-road vehicle. It is packed with modern camping equipment and probably equipped with an electronic metal detector and two-way radio.

For twenty years after the Forty-Niners had their tragic adventure in Death Valley this desert was seldom visited by white men. It was left to the Shoshone Indians who for ages had lived there on its meager store of plants and animals. Then, around 1870, the prospectors began to arrive in the valley. Through the years that followed some of them would become famous.

Survival in the desert was always a challenge and were it not for the harsh nature of the land, perhaps even more wealth would have been uncovered there. Consider, for example, the lost treasure of Charles Breyfogle.

According to the careful research of Harry Sinclair Drago, who retells the story in his book *Lost Bonanzas*, Breyfogle was a businessman in Geneva, Nevada, in 1864, when that young town began to fail and became a ghost town. Breyfogle was no prospector and surely there must have been men who knew much more about getting around in the desert than he did. But he had heard stories of lost treasures, and one day he loaded a burro and set off to cross the mountains into Death Valley.

There he ran out of water and became lost. He wandered for days in the heart of Death Valley, seeking water and a way out. One day he spotted a bit of green up the mountain slope. Perhaps there was water. Breyfogle climbed the slope but found only a mesquite tree growing in the dry desert soil.

He picked some of the mesquite beans and ate them. Then he began looking around, and at this moment he spotted an outcropping of chocolate-colored quartz decorated with flecks of

In Death Valley's early days, a length of stovepipe marked the location of the only well water on the trail crossing Death Valley near the sand dunes.

gold. Nearby he discovered pieces of the rock. He picked up a few and found that they were extremely heavy for their size, heavy enough to tell Breyfogle that he held gold in his hand.

With his gold samples carefully stored in his bandanna, Breyfogle wandered on, hoping to find his way from this fiery desert. He found a spring and drank heavily, then he lay down among some rocks to sleep. He had no way of knowing that he was being tracked.

A little band of Indians found him asleep and clubbed him until he was senseless. They took most of his clothing and left him for dead. Eventually, however, he recovered consciousness. Later he was found and helped out of Death Valley, still carrying his bandanna with its bits of gold ore.

But his mind no longer seemed to work as well as it once had. Try as he might, Charles Breyfogle could never lead anyone back to the spot where he had discovered the rocks so rich in gold. Many have since tried to find the place. Many still dream of rediscovering it; the legend of the Lost Breyfogle has never been forgotten.

Most prospectors went on tramping through the searing desert year after year without saving up much to show for their work. They dreamed of rich strikes. But perhaps they were seeking something else also. More than one appeared to be withdrawing from society. Off alone in the hills there was little to bother them. They were their own men, going where they liked, working when they wanted, making their own decisions. To some, this in itself must have been a kind of wealth. And always, when the old prospector, weary from his day's work, lay down for the night, there was the half-promise that tomorrow would bring a nugget of gold or a vein of silver.

The stories of three other Death Valley prospectors tell us something of the harsh corner of the world they explored, as well as the nature of the men who came to Death Valley in the growing search for mineral riches.

There was a term the desert men used to describe a true prospector such as Frank "Shorty" Harris. Harris himself claimed the title. "I am," he said, "a single-blanket jackass prospector." He had a burro or two and not a lot of worldly possessions to pack on their backs.

Born in Rhode Island about 1856, Harris started West at the age of twenty. His first discovery was made in 1892. That year Harris and a companion, John Lambert, struck gold in the Panamint Mountains, but Harris would rather search for gold than work at digging it from the earth. It is said that he could neither read nor write and did not like business dealings. The claim was sold for seven thousand dollars, and when the money was gone, which was soon enough, Harris was off in the desert again searching for more gold.

Harris, who stood only five feet tall, was noted for at least two skills. First, and foremost, he was successful at finding rich deposits of ore. This made him perhaps the most famous prospector of his time. At least five important mines were credited to him during the fifty years he lived and worked in Death Valley.

Among these was a find he shared in 1904 with Edward Cross, another prospector. In later years the story changed, depending on who was telling it, but the main points can be accepted as fact. Harris met Cross on the desert. They were headed in the same direction so they tramped along together. They made camp the first night at Buck Springs. Harris, as he always did, began climbing around the rocks searching for something of value.

Plainly visible in a piece of the rock broken off by Harris that evening were flecks of beautiful yellow gold. The spirits of the two men soared. They broke off other samples. Then, turning back the way they had come, they retraced their steps to the bustling mining center of Goldfield. Behind them was their newly staked claim and the promise of great wealth.

In town the samples were checked at the assayer's office. This was very rich ore. It promised seven hundred dollars' worth of gold to the ton. Word flashed about the countryside. A small army of gold seekers was soon in motion. Harris, feeling the effects of sudden riches again, allowed the bartender to give him a drink in celebration. This continued until Harris was not thinking too clearly. Then, as the story goes, Shorty Harris agreed to sell his half of the new claim to the bartender. The price was nine hundred dollars.

It was well known that whenever Harris came into any money he quickly spent it buying drinks for anyone who might be hanging around the mining town saloons. With his nine hundred dollars he began ordering beer by the barrel. Later, when his money was gone and his head began to clear, all Shorty Harris had that he didn't have before his gold strike was a headache. That strike became known as the Bullfrog Mine.

Meanwhile, Ed Cross was carefully guarding his share of the new strike, and when he finally did sell, it was for many thousands of dollars. Over the years other desert men had other versions of the discovery of the famous Bullfrog Mine. Several said that they, and not Ed Cross, had been partners of Shorty Harris at the time. Time has passed and many stories have been told.

Maybe the full truth will never be sifted from the tall tales.

But one thing is certain, the Bullfrog Mine was to become the center of one of the richest goldfields in that region. Harris, as might be expected, died poor. He was buried in Death Valley in 1934, famous as one of the original prospectors there. But over those years he had seemed contented. Most of all he wanted to be remembered kindly by his fellow men, and be known as the greatest prospector in Death Valley. These aims are reflected in the epitaph he composed for his own tombstone. It may be read today on a marker at his gravesite north of Bennett's Well. "Here lies Shorty Harris, a single-blanket jackass prospector . . . beloved gold hunter. 1856–1934."

Few people have succeeded in engraving their names on the history of Death Valley more indelibly than an ex-Kentuckian named Walter Scott. Modern visitors to the National Monument find it almost impossible to leave without learning something of "Death Valley Scotty" and the remarkable castle he built in the desert. For many, a visit to this structure becomes the high point of their trip. It was, after all, the only home in Death Valley with fourteen large fireplaces and a swimming pool two hundred and sixty feet long, which was never finished.

Scott ran away from his home in Kentucky at the tender age of eight and headed for the wide open lands of the West. There he grew to become a highly skilled cowboy. He also ventured into Death Valley where he prospected for gold. His skills riding wild-spirited horses brought him a job with the Buffalo Bill Wild West Show, and for eleven years Scotty was a star of the show. During those years the youngster from Kentucky rode bucking broncs for audiences of famous people, including European royalty. The people he met on the show circuit were to become highly important to him in later years.

Once out of show business he turned back to Death Valley, where he still dreamed of finding gold. He always seemed able to arrange a grubstake from rich friends met during his years traveling the show circuits. One man he had met was Albert M. Johnson, who lived in Chicago where he managed a prosperous insurance company. Johnson was said to be a quiet man. He loved Death Valley, and for twenty years he often joined Scott on trips into the rugged Death Valley wilderness. These friends were not much alike. Where Scott was a tough, hard-drinking, swearing desert rat, Johnson was quiet and highly religious. His wife told one reporter that Mr. Johnson never in his life uttered an oath.

The castle they built was a combination of Scott's ideas and Johnson's money. This fabulous building, begun in 1924, cost about two million dollars. Today visitors flock to the castle nestled in the desert hills near the mouth of Grapevine Canyon. It is just outside the north end of Death Valley. Death Valley Scotty died in 1954 at the age of 81. The castle stands as his monument.

In Death Valley, or anywhere, the prospectors who poked around the lonely remote canyons for valuable minerals were often a rough lot—rough talking, hard drinking, and tough fighters if they thought the need had arisen. Perhaps this was the breed of man who stood the best chance of survival in the desert. But one of those who spent much of his long life in Death Valley was always looked upon as a gentleman. His name was Jean Lemoigne, and he was a tall, handsome Frenchman with black eyes and, in his later years, a shock of flowing white hair.

He left his native country while still a young man, arriving in America in the 1870s. After crossing the country, Lemoigne found work in the mines. He saved enough money for a grub-stake; then, with his new burros and a load of tools and food, this quiet young Frenchman crossed Death Valley headed for the Panamint Mountains on the west side of the basin.

His search led from valley to mountain until he came at last to a steep-walled gorge he called Cottonwood Canyon. He found both silver and lead there in promising quantities. Cottonwood Canyon was to be Jean Lemoigne's home for the next forty years. During those years he occasionally left his canyon for supplies. Or he would work in nearby mines a few days at a time to ac-cumulate enough money for his winter food supply, then retire to work his claim again.

When Lemoigne was 77, he was visited by Dane Coolidge, a journalist who told in his book, *Death Valley Prospectors*, of a visit to Cottonwood Canyon. "To get to his camp from Darwin," wrote Coolidge, "I engaged a Shoshone Indian for a guide; and figured that, for once, I wouldn't get lost. An Indian is supposed to know the country, and the Shoshones are reputed to know hundreds of hidden springs which a white man would walk right by. Charley Wrinkle was his name and a more good-natured fellow I never hope to see. Always laughing—but he did get lost.

"We found the Lemoigne mine on the face of the ridge look-ing out over Death Valley; but it was hard to believe that, after forty years, he had got so little work done. It was strictly a one-man proposition." The camp was bone dry, and not only did Lemoigne have to haul in his food on the burros, but he also

Burros survived long after the prospectors were gone and still flourish in Death Valley, where they muddy the water holes, consume the wild foods, and compete with native wildlife.

packed in his water supply. The struggling burros maneuvered the hairpin curves of a narrow, twisting trail along the mountain slope into the heart of the hidden canyon.

As he worked in the holes he had dug into the rocky hillside, Lemoigne thought often of the distant land he had left as a youth. He longed to return to France. The older he became the more he wanted to see Paris again before he died. His mine was worth more than enough to get him back to France. Lemoigne had been offered a quarter of a million dollars for his claim. More than one mining company was interested. If Cottonwood Canyon had been on the other side of Death Valley, and closer to a railroad or wagon road, some said it might have been worth far more, maybe a million dollars. But he had one peculiar demand—the payment, he insisted, must be in cash. Nobody ever agreed to pay him in cash. At the time of Coolidge's visit to Cottonwood Canyon, Lemoigne would have accepted as little as twenty-five thousand dollars for his claim, in cash of course, and headed for Paris.

But Death Valley, where he had lived for so many years, was not to be easily escaped. The following summer, when the sun beat upon the land in all its force, Lemoigne loaded his burros one day and headed down into the valley. He wanted to cross the valley to Rhyolite.

That night he made his simple camp at Hole-in-the-Rock Spring. Burros often leave their camp in the night while their owners sleep, and on this night Lemoigne's animals wandered off into the dry hills. This had happened before, and Lemoigne thought he knew where to find them. He set off on a direct course for Furnace Creek, and there at the oasis were his burros. As he prepared to lead them away from the ranch, the manager spoke to Lemoigne about the intense heat. He suggested gently that perhaps the old man should turn back away from the valley floor and the fiery summer heat. The manager remembered eleven men who had died of the heat and whom he had helped bury. Quietly, Lemoigne explained that he was an old hand in Death Valley. He knew this torrid desert thoroughly. He could safely cross.

But Jean Lemoigne did not make it to Rhyolite, as he had not made it to Paris. Another prospector found his body where the old man had finally been claimed by the heat of a summer day in Death Valley.

Even though Death Valley is now a national monument, there are still mines and mining claims there, hundreds of them. When I talked with the park superintendent, there were two hundred and fifty-five patented claims, claims that are owned outright. In addition, there were about forty-seven thousand other claims registered throughout the monument. The National Park Service has a mining engineer on its Death Valley staff to keep track of these claims. Some believe that Congress should declare much of this federal area an official wilderness, which would erase all but the patented mining claims. Perhaps then traffic into the back country would decrease. Some of the human pressures would be taken off the desert bighorn sheep, and the slopes might erode less where vehicles have run.

Until that happens, the century-old search for precious stones and valuable minerals continues. Weekends bring the prospectors. Sometimes they come prepared to stay. They travel the same mountains once known to Shorty Harris and hundreds of other restless desert wanderers, their eyes always on the rock outcroppings, their hopes of sudden riches always high.

5. GHOST TOWNS

In times past when gold and silver lured the prospectors, each new successful mine that opened had its own boom town. Tents sprang up in the beginning. Miners lived under canvas, and stores and restaurants were also housed in tents. If the town lasted long enough, more permanent buildings replaced these temporary shelters and the town acquired a name.

But the fortunes of the mining companies often changed with remarkable speed and if a mine failed, its town died also. Scattered in and about Death Valley today are still remnants of some of her famous ghost towns. Visitors often search out these quiet, sad places where dreams were born, then died.

On one visit to Death Valley we decided to enter the valley over a route that would take us near Rhyolite, the most famous of its ghost towns. At Beatty we turned westward and drove through the Amargosa Desert. Starting in 1904, this had become a famous trail for thousands of eager people rushing to reach the boom towns springing up around new gold and silver strikes. They came by mule and burro, wagon and chugging automobiles, and on foot. Later there would even be trains rumbling across new tracks into Rhyolite as more and more outsiders came. Most his-

The ruins of Rhyolite, once a flourishing mining center, still stand near the highway to Beatty.

torians believe that Shorty Harris was the man responsible. Mr. Harris found a chunk of ore as rich in gold as any he ever saw and no sooner did word get out than people began flocking to the area of the Bullfrog claim. No one knows for certain how many people lived there when the town was at its peak, but there were probably ten thousand.

As the gold fever spread, new business sprouted in Rhyolite like spring flowers after heavy winter rains. Along Gold Street hopeful businessmen opened restaurants, livery stables, grocery stores, laundries, hardware stores, and law offices. Within a few years the dusty streets of this bustling desert boom town were lined with buildings. There were ten hotels and three newspapers, as well as two hospitals, a swimming pool, and an opera house. Old photographs, brittle and yellow with age, show the buildings standing then. No one seems to know how many saloons catered to the thirsty miners. The number varies between twenty and fifty-six, each said to serve the worst whiskey in the world.

Soon this instant city had its school, post office, and railroad station. Citizens and their families attended church services, socials, and dances, and once even a circus when the big show came across the Amargosa Desert on the railroad.

Among the busiest citizens of Rhyolite were those who made a business of selling stocks in gold mines. Some of the gold mines they advertised did not even exist. Swindlers sold worthless paper to thousands of people around the United States.

In 1907 businesses were failing across the country and a major depression was settling over the land. The demand for precious metals, gold included, fell. Gloom spread along Gold Street, the main thoroughfare of Rhyolite. Suddenly the town stopped growing, and people who had come so hopefully were moving away again. Stores, banks, newspapers, and restaurants all closed. The railroads were soon out of business. Six years after the gold strike that gave birth to Rhyolite, the town had a population of only 675, and by 1920 only fourteen remained. In 1914, when few people remained to receive mail, its post office was finally closed.

We followed the highway to a narrow gravel road leading across the sagebrush-covered hills and up the long, gently sloping mountainside where Rhyolite, the most famous of the Death Valley ghost towns, once stood. A few old walls could be seen standing, broken and ghostly against the blue-gray hills.

Today there are still a few people in Rhyolite. In a tiny white house we met an elderly woman selling gems and rocks to tourists who come by the thousands every year. Nearby, part of Rhyolite's old railroad station still stands solidly where it was when hundreds of people climbed on and off the trains. Surprisingly, the railroad station is still used by another woman who operates a souvenir shop for tourists. They often stop to ask her about the old days in Rhyolite and Death Valley.

Another building nearby is perhaps the strangest ever built in Rhyolite. Tom Kelly was one of the many saloon owners in town, and his business left him with hundreds of empty bottles. The more Kelly thought about those bottles, the more convinced he became that he should put them back to work. He decided to build a house of bottles. His home was finished in 1906, and when he was done, he had cemented 51,000 empties into the walls and roof. It outlasted almost every other structure in town.

Late one afternoon, deep within the National Monument, we found Skidoo, another of Death Valley's famous ghost towns.

Tom Kelly's house of bottles. COURTESY, THE BANCROFT LIBRARY.

Skidoo is marked on the map, but there is so little left of it that it is difficult to find where the town once stood. There are still bits of rusting metal, broken bottles, and parts of broken machinery around the site of Skidoo. Not much else remains. This was the scene of a gold strike high in the Panamint Mountains. In 1905 seven hundred people lived here where today only an occasional coyote howls to the moon or a coal-black raven flies across the sky.

Perhaps people visit ghost towns because they are good places to dream. Stand here and the past comes to life again. The picture grows clearer, and white tents stand in rows along the hillside. The streets fill with miners in from the surrounding hills to buy supplies. Creaking wagons haul heavy loads of food and hardware. The mountain air is filled by day with the sound of the mills grinding the ore and by night with laughter and music as miners wander along the dusty street of the brand new town. The mountainside has suddenly come to life to last only so long as the magic ore holds out.

It is recalled that Skidoo had its outlaws, and the most lastingly famous of these was Joe Simpson. Mr. Simpson went to the bank to take out some money, but because he did not have any of his own money in the bank he took his gun along. In the process of robbing the bank, Simpson killed Jim Arnold, the banker. This brought the sheriff on the run and Simpson was soon secured with handcuffs and taken away. But that night a vigilante group decided to hang Simpson. Skidoo then had a telephone line into town and one of the poles made a convenient place to carry out the lynching.

Word of the killing of Skidoo's banker reached the outside world and soon a photographer was on the way there from the *Los Angeles Herald* to take pictures of the killer. He arrived too late—Simpson was already in his grave. What occurred next did more than any other single act to gain Skidoo a place in history. The accommodating people of the mining town decided the photographer should not have to go away without his pictures. As one of the townspeople explained later, "We just dug up Joe and hung him again and the man made his pictures, then we put Joe back in his grave."

Gold. This was the magic word. Men wandered the vast, harsh desert to the end of their days seeking the riches a good strike could bring, and most never struck it. Ears were sharply attuned to talk of gold and the rumor of a new strike could set off another gold rush. Today the search continues, perhaps more actively than ever, not just for gold but for others of nature's treasures as well.

There are other ghost town sites around the valley. Time and scavengers have completely erased some from the face of the earth. Harrisburg may be a modern city in Pennsylvania, but it was once also the name of a shabby village of tents and unpainted board buildings near the site of Skidoo in the Panamint Mountains. There is even less left of this Harrisburg than there is of Skidoo. No trace remains.

In the heart of Titus Canyon was Leadfield, a more recent mining town. Parts of it still stand, silent and lifeless beneath the desert sun. All that remains are the foundations of a few buildings.

Another boom town in the 1870s was Panamint City, which was four years old when it died. Some prospectors believe to this day that Panamint City still could be the site of rich deposits of silver ore. Robbers were bold predators in this area. They only worked when the mine companies were due to make a silver shipment. Then they met the wagons in a narrow canyon and stole their silver at gunpoint. This continued until the mine owners and the freight line hauling the silver devised a system that frustrated the highwaymen. They cast the metal into balls weighing seven hundred and fifty pounds each. This was more weight than the robbers could lift and they had no choice. For the first time they allowed the open wagons to haul ore safely to the railroad.

Another ghost town is Chloride City, near the crest of the Funeral Mountains on the northeast side of the National Monument. Like so many other ghost towns, Chloride City died young. It died, however, not once, but twice. Beginning in 1878 this mile-high mining camp was for five years a noisy, busy center of gold mining. Those who walked to the crest of the nearby Chloride Cliff could see Death Valley spread out below them with its sand dunes and salt flats. Water for Chloride City had to be pumped uphill from Keane Spring, two-and-a-half miles away, and a watchman patrolled the pipeline, alert for leaks that might waste the precious fluid. After five years Chloride City became silent and its people left. It sprang to life again in 1905, but five years later it became a ghost town for the second time, apparently this time for good.

One of the last of the ghost towns was once a booming new settlement known as Greenwater, on the eastern edge of the National Monument not far from Dante's View. According to Harold O. Weight's booklet, "Greenwater" (published by The

Death Valley has claimed its human victims, and this simple marker, at the end of Val Nolan's trail, warns desert travelers to respect the elements.

Calico Press in 1969), copper was the big attraction. In 1906 and 1907 Greenwater was a boom town.

Some of its events were recorded in an unusual publication started there by two young editors, Curt Kunze and C. B. Glasscock. They came to town with $35.35, started a paper called the *Death Valley Chuck-Walla,* and ran it with a sense of rugged independence. "If you don't like it," the editors advised in their paper, "don't read it. If you do read it, remember these facts: What it says is true; what it does is honest; it will call a liar a liar, a thief a thief, or an ass an ass, as is justified, and if you don't like it you may kick and be damned. Its editors are its owners and will do as they see fit with their own, restricting themselves only in so far as they are restricted by their demand for the truth, the whole truth, and nothing but the truth, and their wish to give the devil his due."

Their paper flourished. Some of its income came from such advertisements as the one inserted by Alkali Bill, who drove one of the earliest automobiles in Death Valley. He ran a taxi service from the nearest railroad to Greenwater. "Alkali Bill himself meets every train," he advertised, "and whizzes you over the desert 45 miles by way of Death Valley and the famous Amargosa Canyon in less than three hours. Better write ahead or wire your reservations if you have time."

But the *Death Valley Chuck-Walla* could not live longer than the town in which it was published. And Greenwater died young, because its copper ore turned out to be of poor quality. The town faded away and its disappointed merchants closed their doors. So did the *Death Valley Chuck-Walla.*

6. MINERAL OF MANY USES

 A *few miles north of Furnace Creek Ranch the traveler sees, off against the hillside, all that re- mains of the once bustling Har-* mony Borax Works. Behind those half-fallen walls with their rusting machines is a good place to begin the remarkable story of borax, the mineral that helped make Death Valley famous.

Borax is one of a group of minerals formed in the vapors and hot springs of ancient volcanoes. In nature it may look somewhat like cottonballs, or sometimes white powder or crystals. Ask a chemist today to tell you about borax and he may list a hundred uses for it. Half or more of mined borax goes into the manufac- ture of pottery and glass. It is used in deodorizers, disinfectants, and salves, as well as for soldering, welding, smelting, and metal refinery processes. It is added as a preservative to cosmetics, food, and glues. Furthermore, borax is important in making paper, ply- wood, and paint, and in the processing of leather. It is included in photo developers, antifreeze, rocket fuels, and dyes. The list goes on, and new uses are still being found for it. There is even a fiber made of borax that is stronger than steel and lighter than aluminum.

Borax had been used for thousands of years for the glazing of

pottery and the making of jewelry. But even in their wildest dreams the desert prospectors who first searched for this useful mineral could not have imagined that it would some day have as many uses as it does today. About the time of the Civil War, however, borax was becoming valuable.

Then it was discovered lying upon the open ground in Nevada. The borax industry began to grow, and as the market for the mineral increased, scouts were sent through the deserts searching for new places where it could be mined. Such a scout stopped one evening in 1881 at the shack in which Aaron Winters lived with his wife, Rosie, in Ash Meadows.

The Winters seldom had much money. Aaron somehow kept

Old Dinah was a borax miner's 1894 answer to the twenty-mule teams. But the mules proved superior and Old Dinah was retired from service. Modern visitors see her on display at Furnace Creek.

them in food and also managed to outfit himself occasionally for another prospecting trip over into Death Valley. Neither did they have company often. They invited the stranger to stay for the night.

That evening the scout showed Aaron samples of borax ore. He then showed him how to test for borax. "Pour a little of this sulfuric acid and alcohol on the ore," he explained, "then light a match to the rock. If it burns green you've got borax."

To Aaron Winters those white samples looked highly familiar. He had seen whole fields like it over in Death Valley. The next morning, after the visitor had departed, Aaron and his wife gathered a few essentials and headed over the mountains and down into Death Valley. Included in their provisions was a small supply of sulfuric acid and alcohol which the borax scout had left with them just in case they should happen on some white ore they might want to test.

At last they arrived where the white cottonballs covered the desert floor. Winters, nervous now, quickly knelt down and poured some alcohol and sulfuric acid on the whitish rock. Next he struck a kitchen match and held it to the mineral. The little flame caught and its colors flickered into a beautiful greenish flame, the most beautiful fire Aaron Winters had ever seen. According to legend the excited Winters shouted, "She burns green! She burns green! By God, Rosie, we're rich!"

Next, Winters packaged samples of the mineral and sent it to San Francisco, where it was assayed by the W. T. Coleman Company, for which the scout worked. Aaron Winters had indeed discovered high quality borax. The Coleman Company paid Winters $20,000 and promptly expanded its operations into Death Valley. There it built the Harmony Borax Works. There was still no railroad to the valley so the borax was loaded onto wagons to be pulled by teams of eight or ten mules and horses.

But the demand for borax grew. There must be a faster way to move more of it out of the valley. According to historian Harry P. Gower, who for half a century worked in and around Death Valley and in the borax industry, the first mule driver to solve this problem was Ed Stiles. Stiles was a wiry desert man, a match for all the mules anybody wanted to hook together. The biggest mule team he had ever heard of was made up of twelve animals hitched together in six teams. But Stiles and his boss at the borax works decided they could hitch twenty mules together in one

Long lines of laboring mules pulled giant borax wagons across the super-heated floor of Death Valley in the 1880s.

long line. When hitched, these animals formed a line more than a hundred feet long. The man driving such a team would be more than one-third the length of a football field from his lead animal. But Ed Stiles figured this could be done as long as a driver stayed alert.

Then came the question of building wagons big enough to haul the borax and manageable enough to be pulled by such a team over the desert and up the Panamint Mountains. The rear wheels stood seven feet high, almost as high as the ceiling in an average room. The wooden wagon beds were six feet deep, and when loaded with borax each one weighed 31,800 pounds, nearly 16 tons. But two of the giant wagons were hitched together behind the mules. Then there had to be a third wagon hauling 1200 gallons of water for the men and beasts crossing the desert. The total weight was more than 36 tons. Each of the mules weighed perhaps 900 pounds. But each animal's share of the load was about 3,650 pounds. These animals pulled four times their own weight across perhaps the hottest desert in the world.

While the wagons were being built, road crews prepared a route for them. Four miles of the road led across what Death Valley tourists today call the Devil's Golf Course. This field of rock-hard mounds of salt with edges sharp as knives had to be chipped and smoothed for the wagons.

This was but one small part of the total trip. The borax mined in Death Valley had to be hauled for 165 miles. Fifteen to 18 miles was a full day's work for mules and drivers, so their entire trip took 10 days. Then they turned their mules around and started back for another load.

As the drivers worked them, the mules quickly became trained to their jobs. Whenever the first pair of mules was led into position at the front of the hitch, all the others would move to their own places behind them. Then they were each hitched to a long steel chain stretched out between them. A long rope connected the driver with his lead team, and by the way he jerked on the rope the driver could tell the animals whether to turn right or left.

Of these mule drivers, John R. Spears, who knew them well, wrote in his book *Illustrated Sketches of Death Valley*, "They were not men of education or very wide experience. Their topics of conversation were few. The driver and his swamper had very little to say to each other. . . . They grew morose and sullen.

The train of three wagons, loaded with borax and water, was hauled through shifting sands by teams of twenty mules hitched together.

Their discomforts by night and their misery by day in the desert heat added to their ill nature."

The roads out of the valley were narrow mountain trails with hairpin curves. The teams in the center of the long hitch were trained to jump over the chain on a curve and pull at an angle to keep the wagon from leaving the road.

The downhill runs were always dangerous. John R. Spears described it in this way: "The load must go down so when the brink is reached the driver throws his weight on the brake of the front wagon, the swamper handles the brake on the rear one, and away they go, creaking, and groaning, and sliding, until the bottom is reached."

If the brakes held all went well. But when the brakes gave way the alert driver had to yell at his team, crack his whip, and set the mules into a gallop to keep them ahead of the rolling wagon as it gained speed behind them. With luck the wagon would reach the bottom of the hill and gradually roll to a stop. But if a sharp curve lay ahead, or a wheel bounced off a rock, the swaying, clattering wagons leaned crazily to one side, often so far they tilted and crashed among the panic-stricken mules. The driver perched high upon the wagon sometimes escaped death in such a crash, and sometimes did not.

These twenty-mule teams attracted attention throughout the country. In the years that followed, a twenty-mule team and its driver were often sent to distant cities where hundreds of thousands of people had the opportunity to see the famous mules from Death Valley. The twenty-mule teams marched in parades in New York, Chicago, and other major cities, and were displayed at state fairs and world fairs.

One driver who often appeared before the crowds in eastern cities was William Parkinson, a colorful desert character, whom everyone called Borax Bill. Borax Bill was a strong, broad-shouldered mule skinner, but rather short. He wore a broad-brimmed hat and around his neck he draped his blacksnake whip. Borax Bill knew his business. He sometimes turned his whole team with its wagons around in the middle of a narrow city street to the amazement of the crowds. For man and mule alike this travel on smooth paved streets with empty wagons must have seemed far different from the world they had left back in Death Valley.

7. INDIANS OF THE DESERTS

 *Archaeologists sifting the story from ancient home sites and other evidence separate the Indians who have lived in Death Valley into* four groups. First came the Lake Mohave People. Little is known about them except that they hunted here perhaps as long as nine thousand years ago. No evidence has been found that these people established permanent homes in the valley.

The Mesquite Flat People, however, who followed them, left behind many home sites where scientists have found ancient fireplaces. Around these home sites were scattered countless tools. It is known that the mesquite trees were important to these Indians as sources of food. These people are believed to have lived here from about five thousand to perhaps two thousand years ago.

Then came the Saratoga People, and following them, about a thousand years ago, the earliest of the Shoshone Indians drifted southward into the desert. Their descendants were still in the valley to watch from hidden places as the earliest white people stumbled unhappily into this desert world during the winter of 1849–1850. To this day, a few families of Shoshones come down into the valley each year, as autumn brings its cooler weather, and stay through the winter months where their forefathers learned to survive the harsh desert climate.

These people lived frugally in the days when the Forty-Niners came into their valley. Starvation was always near. Outside the valley, neighboring Indians were nearly as poor as the desert Shoshones of Death Valley, and each guarded its hunting and gathering grounds jealously. So Death Valley Indians did not rush out to welcome, much less save, the white people who were lost there in 1849–1850. Panamint Tom, a chief of the Death Valley people said to have lived to be a hundred years old, recalled those days of 1849. His people saw the white people at Furnace Creek and could have saved them if they chose. But they did not, and this is understandable if only because of the fear that these strangers would share the scarce food supplies of the hungry Indians.

Indian residents knew locations of every little hidden spring of fresh water in their land, how far they must travel from one drink to the next, and which springs dried up and which ran the year around. Such knowledge was vital to them.

In addition to water for drinking, the spring often attracted food for the Indians. The Indian hunter knew that trails leading down to the springs from the surrounding slopes were places to hide and wait to ambush wild creatures coming to drink.

These Indian hunters had a special way of taking the quail and even some of the smaller birds that came to drink. Lt. Rogers Birnie, Jr., wrote of their methods after a two-month summer trip into Death Valley in 1875. He described how Indian hunters made special blinds in which to hide beside the springs. The hunter would fashion this screen of twigs and grass into the cone shape of an old-fashioned beehive. The materials were carefully woven into a surface that looked natural and was tight enough that sharp eyes could not detect the form of a silent hunter crouched inside. An opening on the side of the blind away from the spring allowed the hunter to enter and once inside have room enough to sit and draw his bow.

Early morning and late afternoon were the times of best hunting for birds, and most likely the hunter was already in his blind when the sky began to grow light above the ridges to the east. When the birds were close to the water and the hunter could see them clearly, the tip of his arrow came silently to the little window through which he shot. The bow was drawn to its full length and the bowstring released. Should the arrow strike the bird and the hunter leave his blind to retrieve his prize, all the other birds would flush and depart in panic. But these hunters, according to Lt. Birnie, had a method for bringing the dead birds to them without exposing themselves to the game. To the arrow was tied a string that trailed out behind it and with the string the Indian drew the bird back to his blind, and inside, without flushing the other birds. In this manner he might take several instead of only one and have enough fresh meat for all his family.

In spring and fall, during the times of migration, ducks sometimes landed on even the smallest of Death Valley pools, and the Indians must have succeeded occasionally in adding these birds to their meager food supplies.

But of all the living creatures of the valley, the grandest prize was the elusive bighorn sheep that vaulted, surefooted, from one rocky ledge to the next. The sheep, too, had to come to water, where they were sometimes killed by Indian hunters.

Sheep hunting was often best done by several hunters working together. There is a report of one such hunt conducted in 1891. In those years there were prospectors wandering through the hills above the valley floor, and the strange activities of the Indians

This pond, named "Badwater" because an early traveler's mule refused to drink from it, is 279.8 feet below sea level.

were soon noticed by some of the prospectors. This story was reported in 1892 by writer John R. Spears.

Their preparations for this slaughter very nearly created a panic among the prospectors that traverse the trails of the desert whenever the weather will permit. These sheep find their feed on the benches and in the gulches of the mountain side, and while eating, it is said, they never look upward. But when they are alarmed in any way, they flee up to the top, and if there be a ridge there, follow it to the highest peak. Having observed this peculiarity, the Piutes build blinds on the ridge-top runways. They started in during the fall of 1891 to build a number of such blinds on crests overlooking several Death Valley trails. The prospectors who saw these blinds jumped to the conclusion that the Indians were building forts to guard mines of fabulous wealth, and for a general attack on the white navigators of the desert. The blinds were in all cases low, semi-circular walls of stone. However, the Indians wanted meat instead of scalps, and when all preparations were complete, posted the best marksmen in the blinds, while the rest chased the sheep up to the slaughter.

Spears reported that thirty sheep were killed by the Indians in the fall of 1891 on the peaks to the north of Furnace Creek. This may have been exaggerated.

Almost anything that moved in the valley was food for the Indians, and in later years for some of the prospectors as well. Rattlesnakes were taken and used as food. It is said that the meat is quite good. Another reptile that was considered a delicacy is the chuckwalla, a lizard that lives in the rocky crevices. This animal may grow to a length of a foot or more and weighs one-and-a-half pounds.

The chuckwalla must be constantly alert because its enemies

The chuckwalla was a favorite food of native Indians. For protection this lizard inflates its body, wedging itself into rocky crevices.

are many among the predators. Color helps protect it, because this large lizard has colors that tend to match those of its desert world. The dry, scaly bodies of the adults are dull grayish-black or olive, and the abdomen is reddish. The young chuckwalla may be marked with reds and yellows, and these colors change as the animal matures.

In addition, the chuckwalla can use its tail as a weapon to strike at its attackers. But most of all it relies on locking its body so tightly into a rocky crevice that it cannot be pulled out. First it crawls into a crack in the rocks. Then it inhales and inflates its body as tightly as a drum, wedging itself between the rocks. This did not protect the delicious chuckwalla from the hungry Indian who punctured it with a sharp thorn to let the chuckwalla's air out. Then it could be easily plucked out of its rocky fortress.

Wood rats were never safe from the hungry Indians. In addition to taking the rat, the hunter would often locate the hiding place where it stored pinyon nuts or other edibles and take these as well.

Pinyon nuts were one of the two most important food plants of the Indians of Death Valley. Autumn brought the season of gathering nuts to the pinyon pine forests up in the high, cool slopes of the Panamints, sometimes a mile or more above sea level. The Grapevine Mountains were a favorite nut-gathering place for the Indians. Here in the pleasant autumn days they not only harvested the nuts, but also hunted for deer and bighorn sheep.

The pinyon pine usually grows about twenty feet high and has a spreading, brushy crown. As the harvest began Indian women used long, forked sticks to beat the trees and thereby shake the cones to the ground. Then women and children would gather the pine cones into the large baskets woven for the purpose and carry them back to their nearby camp.

Next the nuts had to be removed from the cones, and this could be done with heat. Rocks were placed in the fire, and as the flames died down, the pine cones were spread among these rocks. Then, as the moisture within the nuts absorbed the heat, they expanded and forced the cones open. When taken from the fire, the nuts could be easily shaken from the cones or pounded out with stones. This was a long process, and an Indian family would need a large supply of nuts for the times ahead. The nuts were finally roasted for eating, or ground into a flour.

Another important food was the bean or pod of the mesquite, a low tree that grows on the floor of the valley where its roots may pierce the earth for fifty feet or more before they reach water. Mesquite beans were ready for the Indians to gather by

June. The beans were ground into a flour, then the flour, mixed with water, was made into a porridge or formed into a loaf to be baked in the hot sun.

Indian foods comprised whatever the changing seasons provided. In addition to pinyon nuts and mesquite, there were roots, cactus plants, leaves that could be cooked, and sometimes insects when they were abundant. There was never much of these wild foods to spare, and because food was always scarce, not many Indians could live in Death Valley.

8. WILD GARDENS OF THE DESERT

 *In the heart of the sunken valley white salt flats, gray-brown slopes, and canyons of colorful rocks stand silent and barren beneath* the glare of the desert sun. But in this harsh region of heat and dryness, Death Valley has more plant life than visitors may suspect.

Some of these plants are so rare they may soon be extinct. Golden carpet is a kind of buckwheat found nowhere in the world except in Death Valley. It is seen only in the "wet years" and even then no more than a few dozen plants can be found by naturalists in three or four washes. Scientists have a word for plants or animals found only in a restricted area: they call them *endemics*. Golden carpet is only one of the Death Valley endemics. There are twenty other species of plants found only in this hot, dry valley.

The farther up the slopes a plant is found, the more water it has throughout the year. In addition, the average air temperature is cooler at higher elevations. As these conditions change, so do the species of plants. In the salt flats on Death Valley's floor no plants can be seen. But near the edge of the flats there are salt grass and pickleweed, and somewhat farther distant from the salt, iodine bush grows. At slightly higher elevations one finds mesquite, then creosote bush and burrobush. There are zones where sagebrush flourishes, and pinyon pine and juniper grow farther up the mountains.

There comes a time, following the rainy season, when Death Valley springs to life. We once came down into the valley on such a spring day, driving along narrow, twisting roads from Shoshone and over Jubilee Pass through wild flower gardens of orange, yellow, white, and blue. The rains that winter had been the heaviest in Death Valley in many years. Such a season awakens brilliant flowers and brings people to Death Valley from distant places to see the display.

In those long waiting periods between rains, the desert's plants and animals are constantly tested for their ability to survive heat and drought. They have adapted to this demanding life in strange and remarkable ways. The colorful flowers that spring to life are annuals that wait out the dry times as seeds in the ground, until they can germinate and grow. If suitable rains do not come one year, the seeds must wait for another. Sometimes the waiting drags on for many years and in the seed is still a spark of life. Then, with the soil moistened to the right degree, the annuals grow quickly. In a matter of weeks the floor of the desert is covered with the brilliance of flowers.

As the water supply dwindles, some plants, instead of dying, begin to mature and produce seeds regardless of their size. Frederich Coville, a scientist who visited Death Valley in the early years of its exploration, wrote: "When an annual plant is unable to obtain sufficient moisture for further vigorous growth, even if it has attained but a small portion of its normal size, it flowers

Plants, widely spaced, tap the meager waters, and in early spring may bloom in brilliant, colorful displays.

and begins to mature its fruit. If the same conditions continue, it accomplishes the final act of life by transferring its food supply to its seeds, and then it perishes." One plant that he studied grew in wet years to ten feet in length. In dry years it might grow only four inches. But in both years it produced seeds to carry on. In these weeks, also, insects work ceaselessly over the flowers. Then the seeds blow in the wind, lodge in the earth, and begin another period of waiting.

The annuals of the desert sometimes germinate following a rain that provides too little water to bring them to maturity. Desert plants have evolved strange systems of protection against this fatal timing. Not only must rain fall, but it must also fall in the right amounts. Less than a quarter of an inch of rain will cause few seeds of the annuals to germinate, but a half-inch of rain may trigger growth in perhaps 50 percent of the waiting seeds. Some are coated with growth-inhibiting enzymes that prevent the seed from germinating, or starting to grow, until the suitable amount of rainfall has dissolved these substances. Even under the best conditions, not all of the seeds begin to grow. Always, a second "team" is left behind to wait like a back-up squad until another season.

But sufficient rain is not all that is needed. Seeds that might begin to grow following half an inch of rain in the spring will not grow when watered by the same amount of rain in other seasons. Winter and spring flowers of the desert do not get their seasons mixed. Botanists who have studied this desert puzzle explain that a combination of conditions is needed for the seeds to grow. In addition to adequate moisture, they must have the right soil temperature for their species, and this is controlled by the season of the year and the length of the days. Enzymes start the growth only when moisture and temperature are in the right combination. For example, naturalists know that an inch of rain in November and December, accompanied by temperatures ranging between 46° and 50° F., promises to bring germination of the winter desert flowers.

In addition to the annuals, there are the rugged perennials of the desert. Instead of disappearing from sight to hide away as seed, they stand and take all the heat and drought the desert has to offer. Mesquite, burrobush, sagebrush and others, including thirteen species of cacti, have adapted to Death Valley's searing heat and drying winds in surprising ways.

Such desert plants have small leaves or none at all, and there is good reason for this. If they had a large leaf area, they would lose more water than they could replace from the earth, and then they would wilt and die. The creosote bush has leaves that adjust in size to match the available water supply. In drier years it has smaller leaves. In the heat of the desert summer, some plants reduce water losses by curling up their leaves. Mesquite turns the blades of its leaves away from the sun and only the narrow edge of the leaf is exposed to the heat.

Desert plants are famous for their thorns and spines. These help defend the plants against desert animals. Naturalists believe that the sharp projections on desert plants also help protect the plants from severe heat. A cactus spine casts a small shadow, but all of the spines of a cactus plant, when taken together, may keep a large part of the plant in partial shade. And temperatures in the shade, on a hot summer day, may be twenty degrees lower than in the sun. In addition, the thorns and stems slow the hot breezes that might otherwise sweep the surface of the plants and draw off more moisture by evaporation.

The roots of desert plants have also adapted to the desert's underground conditions. Mesquite may send a tap root forty feet or more into the earth where it connects with a hidden vein of water. Shallow-growing cactus roots, meanwhile, spread like a loosely woven mat beneath the soil, ready to soak up any water that falls.

Desert plants are often widely spaced, and sometimes in patterns so regular that the entire wild garden seems planned to make full use of the scant stores of water. Some plants even practice "birth control." In its roots the creosote bush produces a

California dodder is a yellowish or orange parasitic plant that grows on many desert plants, from which it draws its food.

growth inhibitor that prevents young creosote plants from getting started close to the parent, where the water supply would have to be shared. The distance at which this chemical is effective adjusts depending on the rainfall. Where there is more water available, the inhibitor is weaker, permitting more creosote plants to grow.

In the very southern corner of Death Valley there is a tree that has such delicate colors that from a distance it resembles smoke and for this reason is known as the "smoke tree." It is rare in Death Valley, and most visitors do not see this spiny tree with its silvery green color. Smoke trees do not grow close together where they would compete for the scanty supplies of water. The parent tree is usually no closer to any of its young plants than one hundred and fifty feet, and there is a remarkable reason for this. Its seeds are heavily coated with a tough covering that prevents them from drying out in the blistering sun. So thick is this coating that the seed will not germinate until it is scarred and scratched by some outside force.

This treatment comes when a rare flash flood washes down the arroyos where the smoke trees live. Caught up in the rising water with its load of stones and rocks, the seeds receive the rough treatment they need if they are to germinate. If they then lodge in a moist spot they may begin to grow. Research botanists have learned that a floodwater trip of one hundred and fifty feet is needed to prepare the smoke tree's seeds for germination. But a trip twice that long may batter a seed so badly that instead of germinating and starting a new smoke tree, it dies.

Of all the plants, the cacti are most typical of the deserts. These are the water misers of the plant world. Over the centuries they have evolved remarkable features which help them hold the water soaked up through their roots. Their stems are padded with spongelike tissues that in some plants can store a year's water supply. They have no leaves through which to lose water, and they are covered with tough, moisture-proof skin that helps prevent water losses. In many species of cacti, the stomata, those little vents through which plants pass off excess moisture, are not at surface level the way they are in other plants. Instead each stoma is recessed, and in its little pocket of still air it is out of reach of the warm, dry air that might draw moisture from the plant. Death Valley has only fifteen of the 1600 or so species of cactus. Of these only the cottontop, beavertail, and cholla cacti are common.

Arroweed grows in the flat, sandy fields along the road that turns west in the valley to go up toward Emigrant Pass. This is a coarse plant growing in tight bunches. Its roots bind the sands in place, and desert winds blow away the sands around them, leaving the clump of arroweed standing like an old-fashioned shock of corn in a farmer's field. The field stands full of these "shocks" and for this reason is known as the "Devil's Corn Field."

Late one afternoon, when the sun was slipping low toward the desert hills and a haze hung heavily over the valley, we came to Saratoga Springs and another strange part of the story of Death Valley's plants. We parked at the end of the dirt road and then hiked over the rise and down the trail to the first spring.

Along this trail, at the very southern end of the National

Cacti, champion water misers of the desert, can store water and wait out the prolonged droughts.

Monument, we met a young couple with a small child. We stopped to talk and learned that this family comes here often from their home across the mountains because they love this place. But on this day they were unhappy. The Park Service, they insisted, had made a grievous error. They pointed back to the springs and told us that there had been big and beautiful trees standing beside the water, that the trees had provided welcome shade in the harsh desert sunlight, and that people had liked to rest there. "The Park Service had only one reason in cutting down down those trees," they added. "They did it to discourage hippies from coming here."

Later, back in Park Headquarters, I asked the park naturalist about the missing trees at Saratoga Springs. Why were they removed? What were they hurting there in the desert? He explained that those trees were strangers in Death Valley, and they had caused serious trouble for native plants and animals.

Their story really begins about 1823. Settlers in southern California were then bringing in plants they felt would make this barren land more livable and more attractive to people. One of the trees they imported was the tamarisk, a native of the Near East. In California it flourished and people praised it because of its lacy green leaves.

But the tamarisk, sometimes called salt cedar, has seeds that are carried by the winds, and wherever they fall on moist soil they are likely to grow. Once started, the trees might grow as fast as eight inches a week. In addition, the salt cedar is resistant to salt in the soil, which kills some plants. Once it had established itself at springs and along streams, it quickly became a dominant plant. It reached Death Valley in the 1920s and began to grow at Sara-

In the Devil's Corn Field are clumps of arroweed perched on columns formed of root systems and sand. With the sand blown away from around them, they stand like corn shocks on the desert near Stovepipe Well.

toga Springs a few years later. Soon all who visited Saratoga Springs could rest in the welcome shade of the salt cedars.

But these invading trees were doing more than making shade. They were drawing precious water from the soil of the oasis and sending it into the hot, dry desert air as vapor. Naturalists figured that the salt cedars at Saratoga Springs were depleting the water there by at least 1200 gallons every day. In fifteen years the water level in the springs had fallen six inches and was still going down. These foreign trees were doing so well in this new place that they threatened to destroy the marsh which is the home of the endangered little desert pupfish and other wildlife that has lived here for many centuries.

This convinced Park Service biologists that the trees must go, and early in 1972 crews of workers went down to Saratoga Springs with saws and axes and cut down the trees and hauled them away. They return occasionally to destroy any new seedlings that might get a start.

As a result the water has again risen to its old level and Saratoga Springs, with its wildlife, has been rescued.

9. ANIMALS OF DEATH VALLEY

At high noon on a summer day, Death Valley may seem to have no wildlife at all. What could survive in such a land, where the earth bakes beneath the sun, and the searing heat wrings every precious drop of moisture from air and soil? But there are wild animals present and they are not far away. More than fifty species of mammals are found within Death Valley National Monument. Writing in the *Condor*, journal of the Cooper Ornithological Society, Park Service naturalist Roland H. Wauer listed two hundred and thirty-two species of birds found below sea level there. Of these, many are migrants or winter visitors, but at least fifteen live in the heart of Death Valley the year around. There are also three species of amphibians and thirty-six species of reptiles found in the Monument.

The midday sun may drive many animals into their burrows, or force them to seek shade beside rocks and bushes. But when darkness cools the land, the desert night is soon filled with the whir of wings, the scratching of tiny feet across the sand, and the rustling of reptiles hunting food. Kangaroo rats leap about the desert floor gathering their dry foods. Big-eyed pocket mice dart for cover ahead of the ghostly form of the great-horned owl.

Death Valley campers watch for the scorpion, which carries a spiny poisonous stinger at the tip of its flexible tail.

Bats ride the night winds, gathering flying insects. The delicate little kit fox picks its way over its territory, alert for a mouse or lizard on the move.

The lives of plants and animals in the desert community are linked together. The same rains that bring the spring flowers also awaken hosts of dormant bees, butterflies, moths, and beetles. These legions of six-legged creatures are soon moving everywhere among the flowers. Meanwhile, new families of young birds arrive in this time of insect abundance. And as surely as the birds feed on the insects, there are creatures waiting to feed on the nestling birds. Snakes, hawks, owls, coyotes, and bobcats take their toll. Everywhere in this dry world we see lessons in how the desert feeds its creatures through the dry season with its threat of famine.

Some desert animals, such as ground squirrels and pocket mice, face the severe summer by going to sleep during at least part of the hottest weather. This is not the hibernation which allows animals to survive severe cold, but the dormancy of summer known as aestivation. Whether hibernating or aestivating, the condition of the animal is similar. In either instance the mammal has a lowered rate of metabolism, respiration, and other body functions. During aestivation the animal survives on less water than it would otherwise need.

As the aestivating animal drifts into a deep sleep, its body temperature drops almost to the level of the air around it. The pocket mouse's temperature may fall from its normal 102° F. to only 60 to 67° F. For as long as eight months it sleeps through heat, cold, and food shortages without ever knowing what hardships it has missed.

Water needs of desert animals are closely tied to heat and to their eating habits. Like the desert plants, many desert animals are great water economizers. They have evolved to make the best possible use of available moisture, and can often survive on water supplies that would leave similar animals elsewhere dying of thirst. The pocket mouse rarely if ever needs a drink of water. It is out and about only at night. During the heat of the day it stays underground where it is cool, and when it retires to its burrow, the mouse pushes sand into the opening and seals itself away from hot, dry air as well as snakes that might be out hunting for food.

The high-jumping kangaroo rat is among the best-known animals of the desert night. These gifted broad-jumpers are noted for their ability to leap through the darkness, making three-point landings on their hind feet and tail. The remarkable fact about them is that they never need a drink of water. Scientists wondered for many years about the source of the kangaroo rat's body moisture. Some speculated that these desert rodents secretly visited water holes, found underground water, or survived on the moisture of succulent plants. But it is now known that they need not do any of these. Their food is mostly dried seeds. In one experiment they were fed dried rolled oats and barley for many weeks, without any water. But they gained weight. The remarkable kangaroo rat manufactures water in its body by combining the hydrogen and oxygen released in metabolism.

In addition, the kangaroo rat, which is not really a rat at all but more closely related to the ground squirrels, is a water miser. It has such highly efficient kidneys and intestines that it removes much of the moisture from waste materials before they are eliminated. Besides, it has no sweat glands. It remains inactive in the hottest part of the day, hidden away in cool burrows where it does not have to use water to cool its body.

This independence from water means the kangaroos can live far from the springs of Death Valley. In this way the species can occupy a much wider range. But the kangaroo rat's unusual water-making ability is also important to its predators. Bobcats, kit foxes, coyotes, owls, and others consume kangaroo rats in uncounted numbers, and with them get not only the food they need, but part of the water they must have as well.

The kangaroo rat also has large cheek pouches on either side of its mouth. As it scampers around the desert floor at night, gathering seeds and bits of plant material, it stuffs these treasures into these bulging pouches. Instead of running back to its burrow with each bite, it can spend more time searching for foods and thus cover more territory.

As defense against predators, the kangaroo rat has developed a couple of skills of its own. It can execute sudden ninety-degree turns in mid-air, changing course completely in the middle of one of its spectacular leaps. And if that doesn't work, the hard-pressed kangaroo rat may use its big hind feet to kick sand into the eyes of the snake or fox chasing it.

Closely tied to the problem of water is the question of how desert animals manage to survive the extreme heat in which they must live during the hot seasons. For many, this heat balance is the body's severest test. Even the cold-blooded animals—lizards, snakes, toads, insects, and spiders—whose temperatures change with the temperatures around them, must maintain much more even body temperatures than is sometimes believed. Snakes usually die at temperatures higher than 111° F. Lizards perish when their body temperatures climb much above 118° F. These animals control body temperature by moving in and out of the sun, or sometimes by simply shifting their body positions in relation to the sun. The underside of a desert lizard is covered with glossy white scales capable of reflecting heat rays. But on cool mornings the lizard, sluggish with cold, needs to absorb heat. Flattening itself against a rock, or on the sand which still retains heat from the previous day, the lizard warms its body. By turning broadside to the sun's rays a lizard, or other cold-blooded animal, absorbs more warmth than if it were to turn ninety degrees in either direction.

The color of the skin on a lizard's back often changes as the air around it grows colder or warmer. When cold, the skin may become darker. It then absorbs more warmth from the sun. Then during the day as the animal grows warmer it becomes lighter in color and reflects more heat. With these temperature controls the lizard's body temperature may not vary more than a few degrees throughout the day.

Reptiles of the deserts, such as snakes, lizards, and tortoises, possess no sweat glands. They die when they become overheated.

Lizards are active mostly during the day. By scampering from one shady spot to the next, the lizard may be in contact with the hot sands for only brief periods. But the snakes, with no legs, have more body contact with the earth. They seek shade during the day and are abroad mostly by night. A coyote was once observed preventing a rattlesnake from going to the shade. The heat soon killed the snake and the coyote had the reptile for lunch.

Some of the mammals do not use burrows to protect them from Death Valley heat. The blacktail jackrabbit hunts the shade of a cactus or creosote bush. In Death Valley the bobcat also spends its daylight hours resting in the shade of a bush out of the sun's

The desert tortoise is adapted to this harsh world of water shortages and heat.

direct rays. It hunts at night when ground squirrels, kangaroo rats, pocket mice, rabbits, and others on which it preys are active.

Investigators believe that the jackrabbit's large, thin ears, with blood vessels close to the surface, serve as radiators, helping to transmit body heat to the surrounding air and to keep body heat down, making it possible for the animal to survive aboveground even on the hottest days. By resting in the shade, in a depression in the ground, a jackrabbit avoids the maximum heat radiated from the ground and does not need much water to keep its body cooled.

Some mammals keep their body temperatures down by panting. Members of the dog and cat families, as well as lizards and some birds, transfer body heat to the air in this way.

For years naturalists working in the deserts of the Southwest noticed that the little antelope ground squirrel, named for its antelopelike trait of flashing a white warning patch as it disappears, was often seen out in the hottest hours of the summer days. It is the most commonly seen mammal in Death Valley National Monument. Scientists seeking to learn how the antelope ground squirrel could stand the heat so well discovered that if the air temperature rises higher than its body temperature, the little rodent's body temperature also rises. It runs a fever and feels better for it. The closer its body temperature stays to the air temperature the less heat it must lose to remain comfortable. A body temperature of 107° F. may send it scurrying underground briefly, but in a few minutes its temperature has dropped again to 100° F.

Throughout their lives the wild animals of Death Valley must pass survival tests. To live through the long months of dryness for that brief season when there is moisture, some migrate while others hibernate or aestivate. And the weak perish. But behind them there are others to carry on the chains of life, for these species have evolved for survival in the world's harshest environment.

Fish of The Desert

Giant glaciers that came down from the north melted and vanished and left behind a changed world. Perhaps 15,000 years ago, glacial action created a big lake in Death Valley, a lake 116 miles long, 6 to 11 miles wide, and 600 feet deep. But about 4,000 years ago the climate changed and the lake slowly dried up, leaving only a few springs and creeks. In this water some of the ancient fish lived on, right down into modern times. The water in which they lived underwent amazing changes. As the centuries passed, it became saltier and warmer, and the fish adapted to these new conditions. They are known to live in water of 112° F., and in freezing weather they can hibernate in the mud.

These fish belong to a group known as pupfish, all of which are ruggedly adaptable little fish living in little isolated springs and pools in the deserts of the Southwest. Pupfish are small, scarcely thicker than a man's little finger, and in some cases only half an inch long. Their backs are dark gray-blue in color. They were apparently named pupfish by someone who noted that they were frisky by nature and darted around like puppies playing.

Today there are four species of pupfish found in Death Valley National Monument. One is often seen by visitors in Salt Creek in the vicinity of the Devil's Corn Field, where they thrive in

Saratoga Springs, at the south end of the National Monument, provides water for rare, tiny pupfish as well as water birds and other wildlife.

water six times as salty as the ocean, so salty it would kill fish from nearly everywhere else in the world. One subspecies of another pupfish lives in the Amargosa River, while a second subspecies lives in Saratoga Springs. Yet a third species is found in Devil's Hole across the mountains in Nevada in the Ash Meadows area. A fourth species lives in Cottonball Marsh on the west side of the Saltpan.

Modern times have not been good to the endangered pupfish. In the thirsty country where they still survive there is competition for the water in which they swim. Men have drained some of their ponds for irrigation water. Elsewhere insecticides and other poisons have flowed into the water. One species of pupfish today survives in only one pond in Organ Pipe Cactus National Monument near the Mexican border in Arizona. Someone introduced a new predatory fish into their pond. No one knows who brought it in but when the invasion was discovered by park naturalists, several hundred of the pupfish were quickly removed and kept safe in other waters. Then all the foreign fish were removed, and when the pond was ready once more, the rare little pupfish were brought back home and carefully released in the waters where they had lived for thousands of years.

Other species of pupfish are known to have become extinct in recent times. But in Death Valley four species still survive, though they too may be close to extinction. Anyone who has the opportunity to see these rare desert fish should leave them alone and not touch the fish or the water or put anything into the water where they live.

Pack Rats

Another animal you may see, especially if you camp in Death

Valley, is known to naturalists as *Neotoma*. Because it looks somewhat like a rat, it is called a wood rat. But it is unfair to call *Neotoma* a rat because to most it is a much more attractive animal than the average rat. Its tail and ears are not naked, but fur-covered. Its feet and undersides are white and its fur is soft.

In addition, wood rats make interesting neighbors, for they are collectors by nature. Campers living near them often find that small items of their equipment are missing. It may be a spoon, a wallet, or a wool sock. The wood rat travels its territory regularly, gathering up whatever is small enough to carry and not nailed down, and then taking it home. Some desert travelers even complain that they have lost their false teeth to wood rats after placing their dentures near their beds.

Understandably, the wood rat, or pack rat's home can be a wilderness junkyard. Everything it collects is piled around its nest. The home may be built at ground level in a thicket and stand five feet high and measure five feet across at the base. Or it may be a hollow place in a rocky crevice, completely filled with sticks and sections of cactus. Somewhere inside this collection of building materials the wood rat has a little "bedroom," with a soft lining of grass and bark, just big enough for a cozy hiding place. There may be tunnels and runways off in various directions and places where winter foods are stored. But the entrances are blockaded with sticks and thorny cactus parts to discourage the hungry snake, fox, or coyote. Strangely, the wood rat brings the sharp-needled cactus home and seems capable of moving about through its protective mass of sticks and thorns without injuring itself.

There are wood rats in many parts of the country from east to west and north to south, some twenty-eight species in all. Death

Valley National Monument is home to three species of *Neotoma.*
The smallest of them is the desert wood rat, which measures
about seven inches long, not counting its equally long tail. It lives
from the salt flats to the lower slopes of the nearby mountains.
Another is the dusky-footed wood rat, about nine inches long,
found around the Furnace Creek oasis. The other species, the
bushy-tailed wood rat, measures nearly ten inches long and has a
long bushy tail that adds another seven-and-a-half inches to its
length. It is a wild citizen of the pinyons and junipers in the
higher parts of the Panamint Mountains.

All of the wood rats depend on plant material for survival—
nuts, seeds, berries, and leaves and stems. Often they eat what
they find right on the site. Other times, they pack the food home
and store it.

Their young, normally two or three in number, are usually born
in early spring, after a gestation period of about four weeks. The
baby wood rats, blind and helpless for about seventeen days, open
their eyes on a remarkable collection of wild treasures. Soon they
are practicing the fine art of moving small items from one place
to the other. This play is preparation for a lifetime of scrounging
and souvenir gathering. If you are fortunate, you may see *Neotoma* in the desert night hurrying along home with the latest of
a long list of treasures.

Ravens

When you go into Death Valley scan the skies for a large
black bird, bigger than a crow, smaller than a vulture. You may
see a pair of them, soaring high over the valley floor. Or you may

come upon them where they have captured some hapless lizard spotted from their sky-high observation post. These birds of the wilderness are the ravens, coal-black birds of legend and story since ancient times and among the most interesting of all birds. You will know them when you see them. There are few if any of the smaller crows in Death Valley, and the soaring vultures are too large to be mistaken for ravens.

Sometimes ravens are heard before they are seen. Their call is a loud, hoarse, and unmusical "Cor-ack, cor-ack." If you go to Death Valley in the spring, as many visitors do, you may see the ravens stage one of their remarkable aerial shows, because these biggest of the perching birds are skilled stunt fliers. The courting ravens may rush at each other as if intending injury, only to climb and then begin falling toward the earth in a series of rolls or tumbles.

It is believed that ravens mate for life and perhaps this is why they are so often seen in pairs. The nest is a bulky affair of sticks often on some rocky ledge overlooking a lonely canyon. For a nest lining the ravens may collect the fur of dead mammals and fine bark, providing a soft bed for the three to seven eggs, which are greenish-gray and patterned with blotches of brown or purple. These eggs must be kept warm for three weeks. While one parent is on the nest, its mate stands guard ready to issue a harsh warning call if intruders are seen.

With young in the nest the ravens must increase the tempo of their hunting. They scan the highways for rabbits or other animals killed by cars in the night. They search for lizards. And always they are alert for the nests of other birds which they will rob if the opportunity comes. Often when you see a raven, it is being pursued by a host of aroused neighbors swooping down in daring attacks on it.

Bighorns and Their Neighbors

Of all the Death Valley animals perhaps the most exciting one to naturalists is the desert bighorn sheep. The bighorn, however, is seldom seen. This wild sheep of the high places was already in these hills watching when the Forty-Niners tried to find their way out of the valley. But years passed and naturalists learned little about the sheep.

Then, early in the 1950s, a husband and wife team of Park Service naturalists, Ralph E. and Florence B. Welles, began a search for the bighorn sheep. "We could find no one," they wrote, "who knew where to look for them, what they ate, where they had lambs, when the famous fights between rams took place, or anything of the phases of their life history."

As a result the Welleses set up a research project that lasted for more than six years. They located many of Death Valley's bighorn sheep. Of these they learned to recognize fifty-one of the wild bighorns so well that they gave them names. They became acquainted with Droopy, Scarface, Flathorn, Broken Nose, and Dark Eyes. When the Welleses completed their bighorn research more was known about these magnificent animals of Death Valley than had ever been learned before.

The amazing eye of the bighorn sheep, said to be several times as effective as the human eye, is its best warning system, better than its nose or its ears. The sheep standing on a rocky ledge high above the valley detects its enemies early. Then, on powerful legs,

Desert bighorn sheep are no longer as common as they once were in Death Valley.

it leaps from one ledge to the next, scaling cliffs and the steepest slopes, venturing where few wild creatures can hope to follow. It has feet that are well designed for such climbing. Its forefeet are larger than the hind feet, and the hoof pads are soft and flexible but as tough as calluses. They are both shock absorbers and rock grippers, good for bounding down a rocky mountainside in bone-jarring strides.

These magnificent animals have a history that can be traced to Asia. With many another wild animal, they found their way to this continent thousands of years ago when the level of the oceans was lower and a land bridge connected Asia with North America. Their range, when the earliest Europeans arrived in the West, reached from the heart of British Columbia in Canada south into Baja, Mexico.

Scientists found that the wild sheep displayed differences in their physical traits the farther south they lived. From north to south they became slightly smaller and lighter in the coloring of their fur. Once the desert bighorn has reached full size, the males will weigh from 120 to 170 pounds or more and stand three feet high at the shoulders. They are usually brownish gray in color and their hair is long and coarse, not wooly like that of domestic sheep. The tail is short and dark and set in the middle of a large, white rump patch.

The bighorn is known for its magnificent set of horns. Unlike the deer's antlers that grow new every year, the sheep's horns do not fall off but continue to grow. Both sexes begin to grow horns while they are still young and the male's horns may develop into massive ornaments that weigh thirty pounds or more and form a full curl around each side of the head. By counting the rings on the horns, biologists can determine the age of the sheep.

Late in June and into early July, in some of the hottest weeks of the year, the adult bighorns enter their annual breeding season. Powerful rams meet on the mountainsides and challenge each other. Heads are lowered and males rush together head-on. Their horns crash and clatter, but horns, head, and necks absorb the shock. Then the rams back off and slam into each other again.

The females give birth to their young about 170 days after mating. The lambs are born in early spring, when vegetation is green from the annual winter rains. The lambs are born on some high overlook, from which the mother can watch the slopes below for signs of danger until the lamb is a week or so old. Then both mother and young rejoin the group of females and lambs.

Wildlife biologists are worried because the bighorn sheep numbers continue to fall lower and lower. It is believed that once there may have been five thousand or more desert bighorns living in the area of the Death Valley National Monument. Today there may be fewer than five hundred remaining. There are several reasons. One is scabies, a disease introduced by the rancher's domestic sheep. The native wild sheep had little resistance to such imported diseases. Besides, we constructed highways through their range, fences, summer homes in the deserts, and military outposts. And as people move into an area, the sensitive bighorn begins to withdraw. In the deserts, where water supplies are limited, humans have taken over many water holes which the wild sheep had used. When weather is cool, the sheep may get their water from the plants they eat and not take a drink for many days or even weeks. But there are more critical times of the year when the blistering summer heat demands more of their body moisture and they must then find water. Even then they may go three to five days without a drink.

In Death Valley today, the Park Service naturalists talking about the fate of these remarkable wild sheep soon find themselves discussing another large animal, the burro. Old-time prospectors poking around this desert country packed their property and tools on the backs of patient, plodding burros. These little beasts of burden had served people for thousands of years, proved themselves sure-footed in the most rugged country, and were capable of going a long way between drinks.

Their water had to come from the same seeps and springs long known to the desert bighorn sheep. But there is a difference in the way wild sheep and burros use the watering holes. The burros may wade in and muddy the water, or they may, being larger and stronger, drive the sheep from the springs so they cannot drink.

In addition, the sheep sharing the land with burros find less to eat near their sources of water. Biologists studying the Death Valley burros found that burros trampled or ate 97 percent of the vegetation on an area within a mile of one water hole, and 25 percent of the area for five miles around. Such overgrazing permits soil erosion. It also allows plants that have lower food values for wildlife to move in and replace the more nutritious kinds.

Today there are perhaps three times as many burros in Death Valley as there are bighorn sheep. Wildlife biologists fear that the desert bighorns may disappear completely.

10. FUN IN THE DESERT

Where the early white invaders fought for their lives, hundreds of thousands of visitors now travel every year simply for the fun of being there. They come primarily to see what Death Valley is like. In Death Valley on an Easter weekend we have found overflowing campgrounds and roads blocked by traffic. These visitors arrive in all manner of vehicles: school buses, motor homes, pick-up coaches, vans, automobiles, motorcycles, and even bicycles. Most visitors come in winter when temperatures are cool enough for comfort. During the summer few outsiders are found in Death Valley and the national park employees and others who must stay there live close to their air conditioners.

The best place to begin unraveling the history of Death Valley is at Furnace Creek. Here the National Park Service has built excellent exhibits showing the geology of the desert and explaining how plants, animals, and people manage to survive there.

Nearby is the Borax Museum, perhaps the best display anywhere telling the story of borax mining. Visitors can photograph the old vehicles that once were used here—the freight wagons, stage coaches, steam engines, and old railroad equipment.

Visitors often ask the Park Service rangers about desert trails.

95

The following list of walking trips, hikes of half an hour to half a day, lead to historic and scenic corners of Death Valley. Use a park map to find these hiking trails.

Sand Dunes. Leave your car at the picnic area off State Highway 190 and walk wherever you like among the shifting dunes.
Ubehebe Crater. This extinct volcano, standing twenty-six-hundred feet above sea level, is found near the north end of the National Monument not far from Scotty's Castle. It resembles moonscapes seen by the astronauts. Hikers often walk to the bottom of the crater and back.
Racetrack. This floor of an ancient, dry lakebed, about twenty-five miles south of Ubehebe Crater, is reached by a dirt road.

Death Valley scenery viewed by visitors entering the National Monument through Furnace Creek Wash, along Highway 190 from Ryan.

It is here that the famous moving rocks, some of them weighing three hundred pounds, are found on the lake floor. Behind them, like a long kite-tail, stretches a groove in the mud, proving that the wind moves these big rocks across the floor of the old lake. There is a parking lot from which one can hike half a mile east to where the rocks broken from cliffs above do their skating act. Do not move the rocks, but leave them to the winds.

Titus Canyon. This is a rugged, twisting, narrow road used mostly by vehicles with four-wheel drive. The rocky lower gorge can be seen by foot. Leave your car at the mouth of the canyon. The hike is along the three-mile lower gorge, with spectacular rock cliffs.

Borax Gardens. At Harmony Borax Works, start this two-mile hike westward across the salt flats.

Saratoga Springs Loop. This is a one-mile trail around Death Valley's largest body of water. Hikers here have an excellent opportunity to see birds, including waterfowl that have come for the winter. It is important to stay on the trail and avoid damage to the fragile area and the biological experiments usually underway in these green marshes.

Natural Bridge Canyon. From the parking lot on the canyon mouth the trail leads for half a mile to a dry falls where it dead-ends. But the natural bridge is only five hundred yards from the parking lot.

Mosaic Canyon. This area is off State Highway 190, south of Stovepipe Wells Hotel, and it is another of those hikes permitting the walker to adjust the length of the hike depending on his strength and ambition. The half-mile hike from the parking lot at the canyon mouth is highly scenic. But you can go another two miles, or even farther if you want to climb.

Grotto Canyon. From the mouth of the canyon the hiker can negotiate a mile and a half between canyon walls polished by flash floods.

Zabriskie Point to Golden Canyon. This is a three-mile hike through canyons and badlands, starting from the Zabriskie Point parking lot. Those who do not intend to hike the six-mile round trip can make advance arrangements with friends to meet them at Golden Canyon.

The Mesquite Hike. This hike can begin one-and-seven-tenths miles south of Furnace Creek Inn on the Badwater Road. Walking a mile or so through the mesquite thickets, the

The view from Zabriskie Point, named for an early borax worker, displays a tortured, eroded landscape.

hiker is likely to find signs of ground squirrels, kangaroo rats, coyotes, and other wildlife.

Salt Pools. A parking lot at Devil's Golf Course serves as the starting point. There are a number of deep, briny pools a few hundred yards to the west. And by hiking four miles west—and this can be a rugged hike—you come to the Westside Road.

In addition, there are longer trails for the backpacker. Wherever you go on foot in Death Valley, on all but the short walks, check first with a park ranger. The Park Service lists the following safety pointers to help the visitor avoid serious problems.

Take along plenty of water, even in cool weather. One gallon per person per day is a good guideline.

Wear stout boots or shoes, and wear a hat to protect yourself from the sun.

Carry a first aid kit.

Do enough advance planning to determine about how long the trip should take and let someone know you are leaving, where you are headed, and when you expect to return.

Stay out of mine excavations. Abandoned mine shafts may be deep and the timbers rotten.

Rattlesnakes are a hazard. To avoid them, do not step or reach where you cannot see. If you are out at night carry a light.

In addition, the careful desert traveler will carry sunglasses and suntan lotion. Sunburn can be serious trouble.

Many visitors drive to Dante's View, which affords a mile-high look at the salt flats on the valley floor far below.

If the weather is especially hot (above 90° F.) the safest rule is not to start strenuous or long hikes unless you are an experienced desert traveler. Anyone lost in the desert and low on water should find shade and wait there for evening to bring cooler temperatures.

Automobiles can get into desert difficulties also. Engines sometimes run hot and must have water, so be sure to carry water for this purpose. Remember to keep wheels out of soft, sandy places where the car might dig itself in, leaving its occupants out in the desert heat.

Photography

Whenever I visit Death Valley I am up at dawn and out in the hills. In the evening I am outdoors again, watching the changing patterns of the shadows as the sun goes down. These are the best times to make dramatic pictures of the hills and rock formations. During the middle of the day, the sun overhead floods the hills in a flat light. But when the sun is low, sharp shadows give form to the landscape.

Another rule the professional photographers follow when working in Death Valley or any outdoor setting is to shoot a lot of film. By shooting more pictures, you have more good ones from which to choose—those which you will project or paste in your scrapbook.

The sun may be so bright, and the reflected light so intense, that overexposure becomes a problem. Half a stop less exposure can produce more dramatic color pictures (darker). Half a stop overexposed on the other hand may produce a slide too light to have any richness in its colors. It is better to underexpose slightly than to overexpose. Many modern cameras take this guesswork out by adjusting automatically for correct exposure.

Before heading for Death Valley with your camera, purchase a skylight filter at your photo shop. Keep it on the camera all the time. In addition to giving you clearer skies and less haze, this filter protects the lens against scratches. It does not change exposures as some filters do.

Another rule I think outdoor photographers should remember is to stretch the capabilities of their cameras and film. Try shooting the occasional picture you think will not "come out." The results may surprise you and give you your most dramatic pictures of all.

If you have a telephoto lens, take it along. It will help increase the variety of your pictures.

*Photographers find their best pictures early and late in the day,
when low light and heavy shadows give dramatic form to the stark,
eroded landscapes.*

Occasionally turn your camera on small, close-up objects. Death Valley, like so many of our national parks, is a land of big, open spaces, so much so we tend to overlook what is underfoot. For variety and interest include the tracks of animals in the sand, flowers, and other subjects on which you can move in close.

But do not overlook the common tourist attractions. Include pictures of Badwater, Stovepipe Well, Devil's Cornfield, and other famous Death Valley features that you will want to remember. Do not limit yourself. Shoot both the common and the uncommon, the usual and unusual, the big spectacular landscapes, and the little things around you. Remember this and you are on the way to having a memorable set of pictures to remind you of your travels.

Heat can damage film, especially color film that has been exposed. Do not leave the camera in the parked car with the windows up, and never in the glove compartment. Do not leave it in the direct sunlight. The black camera body absorbs heat rapidly and can cook film, causing changes in color emulsions. Then, once you have exposed the film, send it off for processing as soon as you can. These are things the professional photographers remember to do, and they work for anyone.

Sand is another threat to cameras. Grains of sand do no good for the gears and other moving parts. During dust storms keep your cameras covered or in a plastic bag or camera case. If they are dropped, and sand gets into them, it is best to take the cameras to the photo repair shop before using them and risking damage to the moving parts.

Death Valley is a photographer's delight. The combinations of shapes, shadows, and colors give the scenery a never-ending va-

Human figures are dwarfed by the giant shifting slopes of the sand dunes.

riety. This harsh desert world, land of the Forty-Niners and twenty-mule teams, deserves to have its portrait made.

Death Valley Ghost Towns

Ballarat, which lies on the east side of the Panamint Valley, was once a trading town and some people still live there.

Skidoo, which still has some evidence of its occupation, once had seven hundred residents.

Harrisburg was a tent city near Skidoo. There is no longer any sign left of this town.

Panamint City flourished between 1873 and 1877. Silver was the big attraction.

Rhyolite, just outside the boundary of the monument off the road to Beatty, Nevada, was one of Nevada's major cities between 1905 and 1908. Some buildings, or parts of them, remain there today.

Leadfield, which is in Titus Canyon, was built in 1926 and there is still evidence of some of its buildings.

Chloride City can be reached either from the jeep road between Hell's Gate and Daylight Pass, or from the boundary of the monument east of Daylight Pass.

Greenwater was a copper mining settlement which reached the peak of its brief life in 1906 and 1907 when its population rose to more than one thousand.

BIBLIOGRAPHY

ALEXANDER, KENNETH. *Death Valley U.S.A.* New York: A. S. Barnes and Company, 1969.

BELDEN, L. BURR. *Goodbye, Death Valley.* San Bernardino, Calif.: Inland Printing, Inc., 1956.

CHALFANT, W. A. *Death Valley, The Facts.* Stanford, Calif.: Stanford University Press, 1930.

CLARK, WILLIAM D. and DAVID MUENCH. *Death Valley, The Story behind the Scenery.* Las Vegas: KC Publications, 1972.

COOLIDGE, DANE. *Death Valley Prospectors.* New York: E. P. Dutton & Company, Inc., 1937.

GOWER, HARRY P. *50 Years in Death Valley.* San Bernardino, Calif.: Inland Printing, Inc., 1969.

JAEGER, EDMUND C. *A Naturalist's Death Valley.* San Bernardino, Calif.: Inland Printing, Inc., 1957.

KIRK, RUTH. *Exploring Death Valley.* Stanford, Calif.: Stanford University Press, 1956.

LONG, MARGARET. *The Shadow of the Arrow.* Caldwell, Idaho: The Caxton Printers Ltd., 1941.

MANLY, WILLIAM LEWIS. *Death Valley in '49.* New York: Wallace Hebberd, 1894.

PUTNAM, GEORGE PALMER. *Death Valley and its Country.* New York: Duel, Sloan and Pearse, 1946.

SPEARS, JOHN R. *Death Valley.* Chicago: Rand McNally & Company, 1892.

INDEX